OLD WORDS FOR A NEW WORLD

OLD WORDS FOR A NEW WORLD

WALTER BRUEGGEMANN

CONRAD L. KANAGY
editor

Fortress Press
Minneapolis

OLD WORDS FOR A NEW WORLD

30 29 28 27 26 25 1 2 3 4 5 6 7 8 9

Library of Congress Cataloging-in-Publication Data

Names: Brueggemann, Walter, author. | Kanagy, Conrad L., editor.
Title: Old words for a new world / Walter Brueggemann ; editor, Conrad L. Kanagy.
Description: Minneapolis, MN : Fortress Press, [2025]
Identifiers: LCCN 2024020957 (print) | LCCN 2024020958 (ebook) | ISBN 9798889833895 (print) | ISBN 9798889833901 (ebook)
Subjects: LCSH: Church renewal. | Eschatology.
Classification: LCC BV600.3 .B77 2025 (print) | LCC BV600.3 (ebook) | DDC 262.001/7—dc23/eng/20240711
LC record available at https://lccn.loc.gov/2024020957
LC ebook record available at https://lccn.loc.gov/2024020958

Cover image: Compilation of abstract digital painting stock images, JR Korpa/Unsplash
Cover design: John Lucas

Print ISBN: 979-8-8898-3389-5
eBook ISBN: 979-8-8898-3390-1

To Tia, who by her careful copyediting and proofreading has made us both look better than we are.

CONTENTS

ACKNOWLEDGMENTS

I am glad to express my abiding thanks to my recurring trio of generous support: Carey Newman of Fortress Press, wise maker of books; Conrad Kanagy, indefatigable editor; and most especially Tia Brueggemann, a sine qua non for getting this collection together.

EDITOR INTRODUCTION

With some important exceptions, most of my writing is quite autobiographical. What I did was write my way into something of an alternative life. I continue to have to write because it's my way of practicing my freedom. I think it was an uncoerced space in which I could imagine beyond where I knew myself to be.

Walter Brueggemann

As Walter Brueggemann's biographer, I have had the unusual privilege of reading his life and sharing what I've read with many who were reading his work long before I showed up. While I knew that I needed Walter's story, I had no idea how many others were waiting to hear it as well. It is now impossible for me to read anything that Walter has written or writes without the lens of his biography filtering the script. My hope is that those who read his biography will have the same illumination when they read his work. He began as an object for me to study and write about but became a subject with whom my life is deeply intertwined. While we are three decades apart in age, we are both seeing the horizon of our lives in similar ways. I wrote the biography during my best days of living with Parkinson's disease. Now, two years since writing the biography, I am just a few weeks away from deep brain stimulation surgery to try to address the progression of this disease. My personal context means that I've heard Walter and read his life through a prism of knowing that my best days of health are behind me. I trust that perhaps this prepared me to listen with different ears and imagination than I would have otherwise. I trust my stewardship of Walter's story was conveyed more effectively as a result.

As I look back on my early notes from interviewing Walter, when I was just weeks into the project, I see that I was drawing conclusions that an ever-growing mountain of interviews and archival materials never changed in any substantive way. That is, the through line of Walter Brueggemann's story that I discovered early on continues to be the through line I still see and write about. Here's an excerpt from my early notes:

> *I'm beginning to understand some of the variables for understanding the man. Neighborhood and Community. Relationships. Listening, hearing God. The Scripture. The church. His father and their relationship. . . . But these are expressed in so many different ways through preaching, poetry, lecturing, engaging with pastors, and endless writing. In the middle with Walter is God and their dialogic conversation. The energy flows out of what he hears from God. The story of Walter is not a story that I am creating. It's a story that I'm trying to tell as I observe and hear it.*

The current book is a compilation of recent essays by Walter Brueggemann and the third in the Brueggemann-Kanagy series since I published Brueggemann's biography. Max Weber, writing at the outset of the twentieth century, argued that the modern world would eventually find itself in an iron cage of rationality—rules and regulations, logic, reason, empiricism, bureaucracies, and the like. The sole solution to this entrapment was the rise of charismatic leaders who saw alternative realities, named them, and acted on them. The other solution, said Weber, was to return to "old ideals."

Walter Brueggemann has been so effective for so long precisely because he fits the bill that Weber described. He has consistently called on the church to see beyond and confront the realities taken for granted by imagining God's alternative reality. To recognize that the bars of its entrapment were social constructs and could just as easily be deconstructed so that we could be once again enchanted by God's good news.

To challenge the taken for granted reality of the church and to imagine an alternative one, Brueggemann consistently takes us back to the biblical text (the ancient ideals of the church). By doing both he showed us that Weber was right. And indeed, many in the church were emancipated across the past four decades by the courage that Brueggemann showed in speaking truth about the cage and about the alternative to it.

Walter likes to say that "words make worlds." In this book, the essays move between a description of the reality that appears in front of the church and the alternative that God is preparing for God's people. These essays contain an extraordinary (for Brueggemann) number of passages from the book of Revelation that point to the glory to come, as well as from the prophetic texts of the Hebrew Bible that speak to the coming peaceable kingdom.

Perhaps this weaving between the here and now and the yet to come reflects Brueggemann's own status of being ninety years old and having an unusual perspective looking back at church history while being on the cusp of entering the third *E* (eternity) of his beloved German Evangelical Pietism heritage.

And yet Brueggemann is not one to gaze into the sky "by and by" but has always addressed the current realities of inequality, oppression, injustice, and more that the church has too often failed to prioritize. This book pulls no punches in calling out the church for these failures. But thankfully, Brueggemann always follows the bad news with the good news—God! And particularly the sovereignty of a God who offers hope to all humankind and is in the process of calling into being the new heaven and new earth. If words do create worlds, as Brueggemann argues, then the words of this book are an invitation to us to do our part in helping God build that world.

This book offers hope for this life and the next, hope brought on by the consistent call to remember the sovereignty of God in both. Brueggemann calls us back time and time again to the biblical text so central to the pietism of his formation and out of which he has always written. Pietism, with its tolerance of religious differences, its irenic posture, its primary commitment to love God and neighbor, its freedom found in taking the Bible seriously but not literally, and its warm expression of intimacy with God, is at the root of this book. As I've come to appreciate this tradition, I see it increasingly as just the alternative to right and left that, as much as anything, holds the chance of healing our divisions beyond 2024, as it calls us to look beyond the now to the then.

I divided the twenty-one essays in this book into six categories of newness: new community, new governance, new worship, new economy, new earth, and new heaven. At the outset of each part I provide an unpublished quote from my conversations with Walter that connects, sometimes implicitly and sometimes explicitly, with the theme of the essays in that part. I do so because I want the reader to remember that what we read of Walter's theological and personal reflections cannot be separated from the story of who Walter is. Hopefully this will remind us all that our own theology is never separated from our own stories. It never stands alone. It is never static. It is never changeless. It is never linear. It is never systematic. It is always more open-ended and lacks more closure than we are often comfortable with imagining to be the case. But as Walter so often reminds us, the biblical text and the God of that text, neither of which can ever be separated from the other, exhibit less closure and more open-endedness than most of us have understood. These essays, like everything Walter writes, will challenge you regardless of your theology, politics, religious affiliation, and overall biography. But staying with the discomfort will yield the richness that readers have experienced for six decades through the tireless writing of a man who cannot help but write and often, I suspect, writes without knowing what he will ultimately say. And like Jeremiah, the words will burn in his bones until his dying day.

Part I

NEW COMMUNITY

Growing up, my family, other clergy, and other clergy families formed the matrix for my life. I thought that the young pastors clustered around my dad were the most interesting people I could know. They all identified themselves with the German Evangelical Pietism tradition. They all went to Eden Seminary. They all learned the arts and crafts of ministry in the same way. That was my world of reference. It was an irenic ethos, peaceable and wanting to get along with each other, not prone to pick a fight. By and large, it didn't fuss with theological matters. It gave people room, let people get along: love the Lord Jesus, care for poor, sick, and vulnerable people. So it's very simple.

1

MUSIC-MAKING COUNTERCOMMUNITY

AMONG THE MOST elegant, wondrous prayers in *The Book of Common Prayer* is this one:

> *O God, the creator and preserver of all mankind, we humbly beseech thee* for all sorts and conditions of men*; that thou wouldst be pleased to make thy ways known unto them, thy saving health unto all nations. More especially we pray for thy holy Church universal; that it may be so guided and governed by thy good Spirit, that all who profess and call themselves Christians may be led into the way of truth, and hold the faith in unity of spirit, in the bond of peace, and in righteousness of life. Finally, we commend to thy fatherly goodness all those who are in any ways afflicted or distressed, in mind, body, or estate; that it may please thee to comfort and relieve them according to their several necessities, giving them patience under their sufferings, and a happy issue out of all their afflictions. And this we beg for Jesus Christ's sake. Amen. (*The Book of Common Prayer, *814–15)*

The prayer includes petitions for "thy holy Church universal" and for all those "who are in any way afflicted or distressed in mind, body, or estate." But the phrase that always brings me to a reflective pause is "for all sorts and conditions of men." The phrase sweeps across class, race, nation, and ethnic origin. And while gender could not have been on the horizon of Thomas Cranmer, it can readily and properly be added to the catalogue, as this prayer is cast in patriarchal terms. The prayer recognizes that a wide variety of human persons have a wide variety of needs about which to pray; but it also recognizes that in the presence of "the creator and preserver of all mankind," all of these different folk stand in common and shared need of providential care with the hope of "a happy issue" out of all affliction. It is a grand vision of shared humanity in its common vulnerability.

The phrasing of this prayer came to mind when my son, John, sent me an essay by Dave Hickey called "Shining Hours / Forgiving Rhyme." It is from his collection entitled *Air Guitar* (Art Issues Press, 1997). In this brief essay Hickey recalls a Saturday morning when he was eight or nine years old. He remembers that he and his dad, who was going to play music, were "decked out in jazz-dude apparel: penny loafers, khakis, and Hawaiian shirts with the tails out." They picked up a family friend, Magda, "all gussied up, with her hair in a bun, wearing this black voile dress, a rhinestone pin, and little, rimless spectacles that I associate to this day with 'looking European.'" Then they picked up Diego with his bongo drums, "with his thin black mustache and his electric-blue, fitted shirt with bloused sleeves." They were on their way to Ron's house, which was in this "redneck sub-division, in a ranch-style house with a post-oak in the lawn." They were joined by Butch and Julius, who were beboppers. When they arrived, Ron was "barefoot, wearing a sleeveless Marine Corps T-shirt and camouflage fatigues."

This odd assemblage began to play, led by the clarinet of Dave's father. The scene is observed in this way:

> *By this time, the room was very mellow and autumnal. Ruby light angled through the windows, glowing in the drifting strata of second-hand ganja as Ron counted off the song. He and Julius started along, insinuating the Duke's sneaky, cosmopolitan shuffle. Then Magda laid down the rhythm signature. Butch and my dad came in, and played the song straight, flat out. Then they relaxed the tempo, moved back to the top and let Diego croon his way through the sublime economy of Johnny Mercer's lyrics—calling up for all of us*

> *(even me) the ease and sweet sophistication of the Duke's utopian Harlem, wherein we all dwelt at the moment. (35)*

Everyone shared the beat. Everyone got solo time. Everyone was responsible for a particular part. It all came together in an instant of limitless well-being. Hickey is able to see his dad "as the guy who could collect all these incongruous people around him and make sure everybody got their solos" (35). He observes that such a genre of art lacks any institutional guarantee and must "be *selected* by us." It only flourishes in an atmosphere of generosity and agreement, and it yields acceptance and forgiveness. "Kindness, comedy, and forgiving *tristesse* are not the norm. They signify our little victories—and working toward democracy consists of nothing more or less than the daily accumulation of little victories whose uncommon loveliness we must, somehow, speak or show." Hickey observes that such victories are not normal: "Normal for human creatures is, and always has been a condition of inarticulate, hopeless, never-ending pain, patriarchal oppression, boredom, and violence" (39). But artists like Norman Rockwell and Johnny Mercer resist that normal and show us in acute ways, "Hey! People are different. Get used to it" (40). It strikes me that Hickey's scene is a performance of "all sorts and conditions of men [women]," bound together in affliction and in hope.

When I reflected on how it is that *all sorts and conditions of men and women* can come together and make music together, it may not surprise you that I was led to the book of Revelation with its singing hosts. For all our misconstruals of the book, the book of Revelation is a severe, unrestrained act of imagination that traces out a world that is alternative to the stratified world of the Roman Empire, which has reduced everyone to a commodity, and refuses the wondrous freedom and generosity of genuine community. This vision in the book of Revelation is neither "other-worldly" escapism nor is it about life after death. It is rather an act of insistent imagination that competes with and resists the imposing world of Rome. (In our context, that world is now articulated through limitless capitalist greed and unrestrained white supremacy.)

What stands out for me in this alternatively imagined world is the oft-reiterated formula of John, the writer of the book:

> *You were slaughtered and by your blood you ransomed for God saints from* every tribe and language and people and nation;
> *you made them to be a kingdom and priests serving our God, and they will reign on earth. (Rev 5:9–10)*

> *After this I looked, and there was a great multitude that no one could count, from* every nation, from all tribes and peoples and languages, *standing before the throne and before the Lamb, robed in white, with palm branches in their hands. They cried out in a loud voice. (7:9–10)*
>
> *It was allowed to make war on the saints and to conquer them. It was given authority over* every tribe and people and language and nation. *(13:7)*
>
> *Then I saw another angel flying in midheaven, with an eternal gospel to proclaim to those who live on the earth—to* every nation and tribe and language and people. *He said in a loud voice, "Fear God and give him glory, for the hour of his judgment has come; and worship him who made heaven and earth, the sea and the springs of water." (14:6–7)*
>
> *The waters that you saw, where the whore is seated, are peoples* and multitudes and nations and languages. *(17:15)*

This may strike you, dear reader, as excessive repetition for a brief chapter. I can assure you that John did not find it excessively repetitious. He found it necessary and dramatically compelling to repeat the formula as many times as possible and to turn it in as many different directions as he could imagine for a variety of articulations. The phrase "peoples, languages and nations" recognizes *the significant variations in humanity in all its differentiations*, while at the same time its *elemental commonality*. All have in common the dread rule of Rome. All have in common the hope for something better than the rule of Rome. All belong inescapably to the rule of the Holy One who will, soon or late, ever again, override the humanity-suffocating rule of Rome. We can thus imagine a great company of vulnerable humanity coming to terms with the cosmic combat between Rome and the God bodied in the Lamb. John—and this varied assemblage—have no doubt about the outcome of that mighty struggle in which we are engaged. And so the whole company sings in confident doxology:

> *The kingdom of the world has become the kingdom of our Lord*
> *and of his Messiah,*
> *and he will reign forever and ever. (Rev 11:15)*
>
> *Hallelujah!*
> *Salvation and glory and power to our God,*
> *for his judgments are true and just;*
> *he has judged the great whore*
> *who corrupted the earth with her fornication,*
> *and he has avenged on her the blood of his servants. (19:1–2)*

These three articulations come together for me:

- "all sorts and conditions of men and women" in the prayer;
- the assemblage of jazz music makers with Dave and his dad, just south of Fort Worth; and
- the great singing company around John anticipating the fall of Rome.

All of these are glimpses of a common humanity caught in affliction, gathered in hope, prepared to stage, in brief moments, an alternative world of well-being that is an act of defiance and hope. Thus the prayer is an act of hope for "a happy issue." The jazz-making is a respite from a world of work and obligation. And the news from John is a refusal to let the rulers of this world have a last say about our common destiny. So consider:

- the church is a community that regularly prays this prayer;
- the church is regularly a potential host for jazz as the church was the original venue for good music that serves as an alternative to our unbearable "normalcy." It may host jazz as a venue for the freedom of the gospel;
- the church is the primary reader of these scriptural texts, even when they are badly misread.

The church is a host and practitioner of this alternative world of freedom, well-being, and "a happy issue." It invites "all sorts and conditions of men and women" around the news and around the "meal" and may, for an instant, embody the alternative world that is intended by the holy God.

Of course the church is summoned to be at the forefront of these moments of alternative community. It is the church that is called and dispatched to be embracive of *every language, people, nation and tribe.* It is the church that is to be the venue for making glad music whereby we may soar past our divisive ideologies and our mutual processes of excluding the other. It is the church that is to violate all of these old divisions and separatenesses of race, class, gender, nation, and national origin. Thus:

> *We are not divided, all one body we,*
> *one in hope and doctrine,*
> *one in charity. ("Onward Christian Soldiers")*

It is to be admitted that the church rarely performs this task with freedom and imagination. All too often the church is simply an echo of an imposed ideology, whether the false absolutes of conservatism, liberalism, white supremacy, capitalist greed, or whatever. But it need not be this way! It can be a community that refuses all such distortion, and that makes sure that every participant gets a solo part at the right time.

The gathering envisioned in the book of Revelation is not "pie in the sky." It is not the-end-of-the-world speculation. Rather, it is a script for an alternative here and now. This bold imagery of the saints is a defiance of Caesar and every other ideological absolute. At its best the church's singing is not trite or innocent. It is subversive. It gives voice to a *sub-version* of reality that declares *all dominant versions* of reality are false. I reckon that Magda and her companions knew that very well, even if they could not articulate it. That is why their moments together were occasions of grace, freedom, and exuberance—an alternative world indeed!

2

HISTORY IS CLAY

IN HIS WINSOME, page-turning memoir, *Surrender: 40 Songs, One Story* (Knopf, 2022), Bono traces his life story and the way he grew in prominence, effectiveness, and influence. There is nothing of self-serving or boastfulness in his tale, only an account of the ways in which he came to have impactful contact with many of the most powerful world leaders. In his interaction with Mikhail Gorbachev, Bono writes this important eye-catching verdict on the impact of Gorbachev and other like him:

> *So this had been a moment when Mikhail Gorbachev changed his own history and ours. We discover history doesn't have to shape us. The world is more malleable than we imagine, and things do not have to be the way they are. History is clay and can be pummeled or punched, corralled or even caressed, into a whole new shape.*

Mikhail Gorbachev did indeed change the world, surely in ways he had not fully anticipated. The world is indeed malleable, given leadership that is grounded, bold, and caring. Beyond that truism to be derived from the world of Gorbachev, I am especially drawn to Bono's image of "history is clay," an appeal to a most important biblical metaphor.

In spite of our sense of fatedness or our fear of and resistance to change, the world can indeed be changed. In largest sweep the biblical promise is that God is preoccupied with making a new world—a new creation. The most radical promise in the Old Testament is this in Isaiah:

For I am about to create new heavens
and a new earth,
The former things shall not be remembered
or come to mind.
But be glad and rejoice forever
in what I am creating;
for I am about to create Jerusalem as a joy,
and its people as a delight.
I will rejoice in Jerusalem
and delight in my people;
no more shall the sound of weeping be heard in it,
or the cry of distress.
No more shall there be in it
an infant that lives but a few days,
or an old person who does not live out a lifetime;
for one who dies at a hundred will be considered a youth,
and one who falls short of a hundred will be considered accursed.
They shall build houses and inhabit them;
they shall plant vineyards and eat their fruit.
They shall not build and another inhabit;
they shall not plant and another eat;
for like the days of a tree shall the days of my people be,
and my chosen shall long enjoy the work of their hands.
They shall not labor in vain,
or bear children for calamity!
for they shall be offspring blessed by the LORD—
and their descendants as well.
Before they call I will answer,
while they are yet speaking I will hear.

The wolf and the lamb shall feed together,
the lion shall eat straw like the ox;
but the serpent—its food shall be dust!
They shall not hurt or destroy
on all my holy mountain,
says the Lord. (Isa 65:17–25)

This promise is matched in the New Testament with the final anticipation of the Book of Revelation:

Then I saw a new heaven and a new earth; for the first heaven and the first earth had passed away, and the sea was no more. And I saw the holy city, the new Jerusalem, coming down out of heaven from God, prepared as a bride adorned for her husband. And I heard a loud voice from the throne, saying,

"See, the home of God is among mortals.
He will dwell with them;
they will be his peoples,
and God himself will be with them;
he will wipe away every from their eyes.
Death will be no more;
mourning and crying and pain will be no more,
for the first things have passed away." (Rev 21:1–4)

The newness is the work of the creator God. The old world with its failure can and will be terminated. In the book of Isaiah, the world to end is the one governed by Babylon; in the book of Revelation it is a world dominated by Rome, a stand-in for ancient Babylon (see Rev 18). No explanation is given, as we are invited into a world of poetic imagination. Any explanation that could be offered could not be contained, in any case, in our explanatory categories.

The biblical anticipation, this large portrayal of God's radical newness, is in fact accomplished through human effort in small gestures, acts, and decisions. In Christian parlance, it is the *one-at-a-time* work of Jesus to embody that alternative kingdom, so that Jesus deals *one-at-a-time* with persons in need seemingly beyond rehabilitation. It is his remarkable power to make new that is the amazing plot of much of the gospel narrative. Each of his transformative acts of healing, feeding, teaching, and casting out demons is a generative act in and through which the new world—the new kingdom—emerges. Beyond his own work, moreover, he commanded his followers to do the same work:

> *Cure the sick who are there, and say to them, "The kingdom of God has come near to you." (Luke 10:9)*

In the subsequent text of Matthew 25 we get a full index of the work that initiates a new world:

> *Come, you that are blessed by the Father, inherit the kingdom prepared for you from the foundation of the world; for I was hungry and you gave me food, I was thirsty and you gave me something to drink, I was a stranger and you welcomed me, I was naked and you gave me clothing, I was sick and you took care of me, I was in prison and you visited me. (Matt 25:34–36)*

Jesus and then his followers are at the work of performing, in great specificity, the general vision of the poetic promise of Isaiah and Revelation. The wonder of such specificity, moreover, is that it continues and does not grow old. It does not grow old because the old world of fear, greed, and violence continues its destructive force and must be countered—as Jesus countered—for the sake of restoration, rehabilitation, and beginning again.

The specific imagery of Bono, "history is clay," is much used in the Bible and speaks of change for the sake of newness. We can cite three uses of the imagery in the preexilic prophets. In Isaiah 29:16 the prophet use the image to identify the sin of Israel in seeking to perform its own plan in the dark, a plan that violates the will of the creator:

> *You turn things upside down!*
> *Shall the potter be regarded as the clay?*
> *Shall the thing made say of its maker,*
> *"He did not make me";*
> *or the thing formed say of the one who formed it,*
> *"He has no understanding"? (Isa 29:16)*

Israel, the clay, in defiance challenges the potter (God) by demeaning God and imagining autonomy. The imagery is further employed in two uses of Jeremiah. In Jeremiah 19:1–2, 10 the prophet likens God to a potter and Israel to the clay:

> *Thus says the LORD of hosts: So will I break this people and this city, as one breaks a potter's vessel, so that it can never be mended. (19:10)*

Israel has acted in gross disobedience, and God the creator will respond with destructiveness. For all of Israel's imagined autonomy, the potter God will have the last say, and the last say is one of extreme and wholesale destruction.

In Jeremiah 18 the same imagery exhibits God-potter exercising control over clay-Israel. It can go either way with the potter, as the potter has complete freedom (vv. 7–10). But the verdict of Jeremiah concerns a potter who has lost patience and will "shape evil" and "devise a plan" that in context is defined by Babylon:

> *Look, I am a potter shaping evil against you and devising a plan against you. Turn now, all of you, from your evil ways, and amend your ways and your doings. (Jer 18:11)*

In the exilic and postexilic texts, the imagery is inverted and made positive. In Lamentations 4:2, the "worth" of Israel is assessed. It is affirmed that in truth Israel is "worth its weight in gold." In the happenstance of history, however, Israel's true worth is not recognized as it is treated as nearly worthless, like a clay pot that is readily discarded. Thus the lament opines that Israel's true worth goes unrecognized in the world of the great powers, perhaps like Latvia or Estonia, too readily disregarded and discounted by the major powers.

The imagery recurs in three texts in later Isaiah. The usage in Isaiah 41:25 contemplates the rise of Persian power that will "trample" Babylon like a potter treads clay. Thus mighty Babylon is made vulnerable to the assault of Persia. The image in Isaiah 45:9 echoes 29:16 as the way in which the pot questions the potter:

> *Woe to you who strive with your Maker,*
> *Earthen vessels with the potter!*
> *Does the clay say to the one who fashions it, "What are you making?"*
> *or "Your work has no handles?"*

The pot is pictured as asking questions about the work of the potter. It is not, however, the right or the prerogative of the pot to question the potter. Thus Israel questions YHWH's intent to deliver exiled Israel by the hand of Cyrus the Persian. It is as though Israel is objecting to YHWH's intent, a completely inappropriate response. It is the proper role of the clay to keep turning on the wheel at the behest of the potter. So it is Israel's proper business to receive willingly what YHWH decrees. The matter is reinforced in verse 10, wherein the fetus questions the father or mother in a wholly inappropriate way:

> *Woe to anyone who says to a father, "What are you begetting?"*
> *or to a woman, "With what are you in labor?"*

In the imagery of both verses 9 and 10 Israel has forgotten that it is subject to the will of the creator God and has no ground from which to raise objection.

Finally, in Isaiah 64:8 the imagery occurs in a lament wherein Israel helpless and vulnerable, and has no recourse except to rely on the potter God for well-being. The lament, however, suggests that the potter God has been "exceedingly angry," and that Israel is without any hope at all (v. 9). Its only hope is to rely on the potter-God whose construct it is. These several uses altogether attest that the image of potter-pot can serve in a variety of ways to articulate the proper relationship of God and Israel. The insistence in all of these uses is that YHWH holds initiative for the life and history of Israel, and Israel must receive from YHWH the life and history that YHWH intends.

This same imagery has a dramatic usage in the New Testament. In Paul's tricky, complex argument about the role of Israel in God's intention for salvation Paul writes about God's freedom to show compassion (Rom 9:15) to insist that all of human history depends on God's mercy (v. 16). God's free dispatch of Israel and the community of Christ is according to God's freedom, which is beyond human questioning:

> *But who indeed are you, a human being, to argue with God? Will what is molded say to the one who molds it, ""Why have you made me like this?" Has the potter no right over the clay, to make out of the same lump one object for special use and another for ordinary use? (Rom 9:20–21)*

Again the imagery affirms and insists that God's authoritative priority to which human creatures must willingly assent. And in God's freedom much is possible that otherwise could not be. And now Paul utilizes that imagery to assert that the way of God in human history is supple, pliable, and plastic.

We may be left with two important questions. First, who is it that imagines that human history cannot be "pummeled, punched, corralled or caressed into a wholly new shape"? No doubt there are two such populations. On the one hand those who doubt that history is pliable are *those who are left in hopelessness and despair*, who do not believe that history can be changed for the better. On the other hand, the same conclusion may be reached by *the strongly advantaged* who have a great stake in present world arrangements, and readily can see than any change will mean their loss. But the future openness of history does not depend on either those lost in despair or those lost in advantage. It depends on those who are willing and able to be pliable clay that will yield to the purposeful will of the creator God. Bono—and Gorbachev—are clearly among those who are both willing recipients and willing agents of the purposeful change intended by the creator.

The second question concerns the agency of change. On the one hand, there are those who *abdicate and resign*, who can say too easily, "God's got this," as though God were a completely isolated and lonely agent. On the other hand, there are those who *easily conclude that "God has no hands but our hands,"* as though it were all up to us. Biblical faith is of another ilk and rejects both resignation and human autonomy. Such faith has no doubt that God's large intention—voiced by the poets—does indeed bend history toward justice, mercy, and compassion. But such faith also affirms that human investment in justice, mercy, and compassion is of utmost urgency. Variously in the tradition we may, as with John Calvin, get an accent on divine governance, or as with John Wesley get an emphasis on human agency. But biblical faith never chooses between the two, and celebrates the prospect that human insistence may be fully in sync with the abiding purposes of God.

Thus may savor the verdict of Bono, "history is clay," and see that his statement comes at the end of a long line of witnesses who have run risks so that the old world may finally be the world that God, the creator, intends. Or to put it in the form of a doxology,

> *The kingdom of the world has become the kingdom of our Lord*
> *and of his Messiah,*
> *and he will reign forever and ever. (Rev 11:15)*

The apocalyptic vision is grand and sweeping. It depends, however, on the daily work to bring the vision to actuality.

I may conclude with the wisdom of Peter Berger and Thomas Luckmann in *The Social Construction of Reality: A Treatise in the Sociology of Knowledge* (Doubleday, 1967). From a sociological perspective they write,

> *It should be clear from the foregoing that the statement that man produces himself in no way implies some sort of Promethean vision of the solitary individual. Man's self-production is always and of necessity, a social enterprise. Men together produce a human environment, with the totality of its socio-cultural and psychological formations. None of these formations may be understood as products of man's biological constitution, which, as indicated, provide only the outer limits for human productivity. Just as it is impossible for man to develop as man in isolation, so it is impossible for man in isolation to produce a human environment. (51)*

Berger and Luckmann write as sociologists, so their horizon is of necessity limited to human community. A different kind of interpreter might also include the agency of God in the community that may produce a livable environment. In order for such a social enterprise to matter decisively, it aims at transformation. And transformation happens as "the individual switches worlds" (156–57). It is the human work of nurture, education, pastoral attentiveness, and liturgy to empower individual persons to "switch worlds." In the time of Jesus it was a switch from the world of Rome to that of covenant. In our time it is perhaps to "switch worlds" from the governance of Mammon to the rule of God (Matt 6:24). *Mammon* is at work daily in world construction. But so also *the community of covenantal justice and mercy* is at work world-making. We are invited, along with Bono, to sign on with the pummeling, punching, corralling, and caressing work of a new shape for well-being. This is the good work the creator intends. This is the good work that Jesus fully embodied.

Before we finish, we may pause to sing:

Spirit of the living God, fall afresh on me.
Spirit of the living God, fall afresh on me.
Melt me, mold me, *fill me, use me.*
Spirit of the living God, fall afresh on me.

Glory to God *288 (Daniel Iverson, 1926)*

3

THE DANGEROUS ARSON OF A BRAMBLE

I WAS ORDAINED in 1958 alongside my brother Ed. He promptly accepted a pastoral call to St. Paul Church in Napoleon, Missouri. It was a small rural parish. Soon after he arrived at the church, he learned that the Women's Guild of the congregation had a "wee leadership crisis." They could not find anyone in their group who would accept leadership for the guild. The chair of the nominating committee for the guild reported, "We have asked everyone, and no one would agree to serve." The story becomes poignant because a somewhat disgruntled woman in the group said in a stage whisper, "They did not ask everyone." That is, they did not ask her, because they judged her ill-suited for such leadership.

This slight memory from my brother, Ed, has caused me to turn to the parable about leadership in Judges 9:8–15. In that parable told by Jotham, youngest son of Gideon (=Jerubbaal), the trees wanted to anoint a king over them. The olive tree declined kingship, and wanted instead to continue to produce rich oil. The fig tree likewise declined kingship, preferring to produce the sweetness of figs. And the grape vine declined, wanting only to continue to produce grapes for wine. All of these trees—olive, fig, and vine—were too busy with their productive work to accept the demanding role of governance. When all of the candidates declined kingship, the bramble volunteered to occupy the vacancy. The bramble accepted the role of king, but stated a stark either/or for governance:

> *If in good faith you are anointing me king over you,*
> *then come and take refuge in my shade;*

but if not, let the fire come out of the bramble
and devour the cedars of Lebanon. (Judg 9:15)

My way or fire! If the other trees trusted the bramble, all would be well. If not, the bramble promised a destructive fire.

The parable is rather obvious and does not require much commentary. Dennis Olson, in his fine commentary (*NIB* 2), gives the parable itself only seventeen lines (p. 816). The point of the parable is that if good people will not provide leadership, the vacuum will be filled by those less effective and less responsible. I thought perhaps that the leadership crisis in Napoleon, Missouri is a case in point for the parable.

In the book of Judges the parable is set in an extended narrative that concerns the governance of Gideon-Jerubbaal and what comes after him. As judge and savior of Israel, Gideon delivered the Israelites from the Midianite threat with a great victory. In their gratitude the people of Israel offered Gideon kingship with the continuing right of his family after him. Gideon nobly refuses the offer:

I will not rule over you, and my son will not rule over you;
the Lord will rule over you. (8:23)

Upon the death of Gideon, his son Abimelech steps forward as successor to his father, and ruthlessly kills his many brothers, sons of Gideon, who might have shared power with him. By popular acclaim, Abimelech is made king, appointed to the office his father had generously declined, an office never heretofore present in Israel. He becomes the first king in Israel, well before either Saul or David was on the horizon. While Abimelech killed all of his brothers but one, Jotham, the youngest, had somehow survived. Young Jotham mounts a protest against the usurpatious rule of his brother and utilizes the parable in order to identify the rule of Abimelech as evil and sure to fail. After reciting the parable, Jotham had to flee for his life from his brother Abimelech, now made king.

The remainder of this restless story of Abimelech is told, governed by "an evil spirit" dispatched by God (9:23). Abimelech lasted in power only three years. As a counterpoint to the threat of fire voiced by the bramble in the parable, Abimelech with his troops gathers brushwood and sets the Tower of Shechem aflame:

> *So every one of his troops cut down a bundle and following Abimelech put it against the stronghold, and they set the stronghold on fire over them, so that all the people of the Tower of Shechem also died, about a thousand men and women. (v. 49)*

As a reprise he also attempts to set fire to the strong tower of Thebez (vv. 50–51). While he was busy working on that fire, a woman from up on the tower threw a millstone down on him and crushed his skull. Thus he died, shamefully killed by a woman! The narrative concludes with a verdict that the violent end of Abimelech was God's revenge for his violent murder of his brothers:

> *Thus God repaid Abimelech for the crime he committed against his father in killing his seventy brothers; and God also made all the wickedness of the people of Shechem fall back on their heads, and on them came the curse of Jotham son of Jerubbaal. (9:56–57)*

The curse uttered by Jotham in the form of the parable has now come to fruition. Thus from *the "evil spirit"* of verse 23 to *the vengeance of God* in verses 56–57, the whole of the life and rule of Abimelech is contained in the governance of God, a containment about which he knew nothing. God will not be mocked by violent, self-serving governance. Abimelech is deposed and the narrative of Judges moves on to the emergent rule of Jephthah to face the next crisis, this one from the Ammonites.

Back in Shechem, the rule of YHWH trumped the evil rule of Abimelech. The parable is a warning about *poor leadership* that can do *great harm to the body politic.* Back in Napoleon, what was perceived to be potentially poor leadership was refused. My comment, however, does not concern the leadership crisis in either ancient Shechem or in Napoleon. Rather, it concerns the stunning fact that in my home state of Michigan the leadership of the Republican Party has been completely preempted by Trumpian folk who continue to claim that the election of 2020 was rigged and that Biden is not our legitimately elected president. These Republican leaders in fact have no interest in governance; they are quite willing to devote their energy and attention solely to conspiracy theories that refuse the political realities of our state. What is happening in Michigan, moreover, is happening more broadly across our nation, thus creating a leadership crisis and thereby placing our democratic institutions and procedures in jeopardy.

I call attention to the parable of Jotham because it is so readily accessible, and so easily pertinent to our current political crisis. When good leadership does not step up to responsibility, it may go by default to nefarious control of others who intend no positive outcome for the common good. This political reality, read through the lens of this biblical parable, is yet another cogent reminder to us that gospel faith is concerned with the real world of governance and is not confined to matters spiritual or other-worldly. It may well be that the church (and its leadership) are regularly cast as "talent scouts" to identify potential local leaders, to recruit them for public office, and to school them in the ways in which the gospel concerns civic realism. Abimelech may have claimed for himself the title of king. But he had no real interest in or capacity for governance.

The great temptation in governance is always the chance for self-benefit. Thus even though Gideon refused kingship, he acted nonetheless in covetous ways:

> *"Let me make a request of you; each of you give me an earring he has taken as booty." (For the enemy had golden earrings, because they were Ishmaelites.) "We will willingly*

> *give them," they answered. So they spread a garment, and each threw into it an earring he had taken as booty. The weight of the golden earrings that he requested was one thousand seven hundred shekels of gold (apart from the crescents and the pendants and the purple garments worn by the kings of Midian, and the collars that were on the necks of their camels). (Judg 8:24–26)*

In the next verse we are told, moreover, that Gideon engaged with religious symbols (*ephod*) that the narrator identifies as a "snare" whereby Gideon and all Israel "prostituted themselves" (v. 27). This report juxtaposes self-serving political practice (greed) and destructive religious practice (idolatry) that characteristically come together.

In ancient Israel the construction of kingship was in crisis as the occupant of the royal office variously adjudicated public interest and private gain. It remained for the hard-nosed old judge Samuel to enunciate the risks of concentrated power in the hands of a bramble-like leader:

> *There will be the ways [*mišpat*] of the king who will reign over you: he will take your sons and appoint them to his chariots and to be his horsemen and to run before his chariots; and he will appoint for himself commanders of thousands and commanders of fifties, and some to plow his ground and to reap his harvest, and to make his implements of war and the equipment of his chariots. He will take your daughters to be perfumers and cooks and bakers. He will take the best of your fields and vineyards and olive orchards and give them to his courtiers. He will take one-tenth of your grain and of your vineyards and give it to his officers and his courtiers. He will take your male and female slaves, and the best of your cattle, and donkeys, and put them to his work. He will take one-tenth of your flocks, and you shall be his*

> *slaves. And in that day you will cry out because of your king, whom you have chosen for yourselves; but the LORD will not answer you in that day. (1 Sam 8:11–18)*

It remained, in the modern world, for Machiavelli to line out this reality of public power of *The Prince*. The episode of Abimelech in ancient Israel permits the narrator to assert the deep learning that human governance is always penultimate and answerable to the ultimate governance of God. That lesson is one we always seem to relearn belatedly. My guess is that the women in the church in Napoleon had fully intuited this reality, even if they did not and could not spell it out. They knew, as we always learn again, that sooner or later brambles will burn the house down. Thus we might recall the towers of Shechem and Thebez in the time of Abimelech, and then we may ponder the wise words of Paul Krugman, "Blackmailers without a Cause," *New York Times* (February 3, 2023):

> *It's dangerous when a political party is willing to burn things down unless it gets it way; it's even more dangerous when that party just wants to watch thing burn.*

Brambles are relentless when they do not get their way!

Part II

NEW GOVERNANCE

I don't like to be pigeonholed. I utilize categories but resist them at the same time. I see this not as contradictory but complementary because it keeps the dialectic open-ended and unsettled. This is a way of not arriving in a box. That's particularly true of my location in the church. Evangelicals certainly think I'm a progressive, but I am very suspect among many progressives. And that's a place where I like to be. I am suspect among progressives because I stay very close to the Bible. I count on the old formula that progressives regard as obsolete and passe. That formula is that we are saved by grace alone. Progressives believe that God has no hands but our hands. I am very much in the wake of Reinhold Niebuhr who in our tradition taught me a great deal about how to do that juggling that that he does so well. I would regard and be regarded by Pentecostals as a traveling companion because, as you know, Pentecostals are not stuck in all the old Reformation categories either. I think that what the Pentecostals call the work of the spirit, is what I call the work of imagination.

4

BEYOND THE GOVERNOR'S ILLUSION

I REMEMBER IN the sixth grade that we studied US history.* This was in 1944; D-Day had happened successfully. The Allies were on their way, step-by-step, to victory in Berlin. I read the newspaper every day to see how many miles General Patton and his army had advanced. By that time we all had confidence in a soon-coming Allied victory. In our study we learned the names of the presidents of the United States. We did not differentiate among them. I put them all on a handsome chart, including the wars they had won and the church to which each one belonged. (I can still recite that roster, though sometimes I forget to mention Millard.) I also made a wondrous poster of our several "five-star" heroes of the day:

- Army generals: Eisenhower, MacArthur, Marshall;
- Air Force general: Arnold;
- Navy admirals: King, Leahy, Nimitz.

It was all unreservedly positive, going from victory to victory, with no doubt of our own contribution to the war effort and no doubt of the rightness of the cause. Nobody noticed or bothered to tell us that our roster of heroes was exclusively white and male.

But I also remember that in seminary our beloved teacher, Allen Wehrli, walked us through 1 and 2 Kings. He helped us to see that the writer of this text cited source materials:

* In memory of the well-beloved Charlie Cousar, who first taught me about Matthew 27:65.

> *Now the rest of the acts of Jeroboam, how he warred and how he reigned, are written in the Book of the Annals of the Kings of Israel (1 Kings 14:19).*
>
> *The rest of the acts of Abijam, and all that he did, are they not written in the Book of the Annals of the Kings of Judah? (1 Kings 15:7)*

He helped us see that this "biblical history" was a certain kind of history that had been written in a very different way from the one offered by the sources he cited. By this he made clear that the biblical rendering of the past of Israel and Judah was just one of many possible renderings, and it was a very peculiar rendering that featured very different "historical players." The writer who cited these sources also let us know there were many other data in which he, the biblical historian, had no interest and he was not going to cite this material. Amid the tedium of the recital of the many kings of Israel and Judah, it was clear (as Gerhard von Rad later showed so well) that history relentlessly depended on the word of God and not the will of kings. The royal recitals were, moreover, variously interrupted in order to include narrative pauses for the inexplicable and disruptive appearance of Elijah (1 Kings 17–21), Elisha (2 Kings 2–9), Micaiah (1 Kings 22), and Isaiah (2 Kings 18–20). This history turned out to be very different from and much less triumphant than the ordinary rendering of US history that I learned in the sixth grade. Indeed this history ended in 2 Kings 25 with deportation, with a last surviving member of the Davidic house under surveillance in Babylon. The contrast between my sixth grade learning and my seminary learning was spectacular. The first was unmitigatedly triumphant; the second was shrewdly deabsolutizing in order to make room for the divine purpose and for renegade outsiders. A reinforcement of attentiveness to the difference was the appearance in 1980 of the book by Howard Zinn, *A People's History of the United States, 1492 to the Present.* Zinn showed that history could be written "from below," without preoccupation with presidents and victories.

And now comes Governor DeSantis of Florida, who wants to return to the simplicity of my sixth-grade US history, wherein our past is an unambiguous recital of victories, all accomplished by male white persons whom he would label as "Christian." DeSantis wants to have excluded from our memory any positive mention of those who conducted our history "from below," all the nonwhites who have insisted on justice and who created our national wealth. Beyond that he wants to eliminate critical thinking under the guise of banning "critical race theory" (whatever that may mean, though I am certain he has no clear idea). He has proposed that no child should be taught anything that makes them uncomfortable—that is, anything that disrupts the simplistic, nostalgic memory of white domination, a view preferred by the parents that support him.

Of course the thinking of the Florida governor is completely in line with how governors (and other people in power) are wont to think. Pilate, the Roman governor, whom we mention in the creed under the rubric of state execution ("crucified under Pontius Pilate"), sought to make the tomb of the executed Jesus safe from body-stealing. He instructed the soldiers under his command concerning the tomb,

> *You have a guard of soldiers; go, make it as secure as you can. (Matt 27:65)*

The narrator adds,

> *So they went with the guard and made the tomb secure by sealing the stone. (v. 66)*

Like the Roman governor, the Florida governor wants to make US history "as secure as you can." Make it safe from shame. Make it safe from embarrassment. Make it safe by sidelining Native Americans and Black people, so make it safely white. Make it safe by a failure to mention slavery. Make it safe by a refusal to notice genocide. The

Roman governor had immense power, and so he believed he could contain the executed body of the dead Jesus. The Florida governor has immense power, so he believes he can contain the violence and shame and embarrassment of our national history. Pilate only needed attentive soldiers. DeSantis only needs reliable censors (parents!) and docile teachers who adhere to the state program of silence and exclusion.

But of course the Roman governor did not succeed in his "security." After his instruction in Matthew 27:65, only three verses later we get this:

> *And suddenly there was a great earthquake; for an angel of the Lord, descending from heaven, came and rolled back the stone and sat on it. His appearance was like lightning, and his clothing white as snow. For fear of him the guards shook and became like dead men. But the angel said to the women, "Do not be afraid; I know that you are looking for Jesus who was crucified. He is not here; he has been raised as he said. Come, see the place where he lay." (28:2–6)*

The governor's plan had malfunctioned. His illusion of imperial power could not prevail. And now we will see if the Florida governor can prevail in his fear-filled design. Likely not. Likely not because the truth cries out from the blood-soaked ground, the truth of Black servitude and Native American genocide. It is the truth of hate and violence and fear, of hope and resilience. It turns out, against every governor's hope for "safe and secure," that history is relentlessly kept open by the inscrutable purposes of God that defy every human reductionism.

The church has a huge stake in this matter. The church knows very well, in the wake of the resurrection of Jesus, that historical processes are open-ended and cannot be closed off by our fear, or our clever management, or our all-knowing technology. It is the good work of the church to witness, in every season, to the openness of the historical process to the incursions of God's newness on behalf of justice, mercy, and compassion. Thus every "strong man" comes to a sad ending. Every state that majors in control and surveillance is overthrown. Every attempt at racial domination faces challenges that it cannot finally put down.

So let the local congregation, week by week, pay attention to the newness that surges among us that is sometimes seen as emancipation, and more often seen as disruption. Let the church notice newness that is local through a gesture, a word, or an act. Let the local church provide and celebrate a regular index of the emancipatory surprises amid the historical process, of a bold woman with a new initiative, of a prayer for rain answered, of an act of holiness, or compassion, or imagination. Or let the church take notice of a life beyond exploitation that makes our management quite penultimate—of a drought or a mudslide, or a bloodletting. We can, as we like, sing with hope and confidence:

What a fellowship, what a joy divine,
Leaning on the everlasting arms;
What a blessedness, what a peace is mine,
Leaning on the everlasting arms,
Leaning, leaning,
Safe and secure from all alarms
Leaning, leaning,
Leaning on the everlasting arms.
Oh, how sweet to walk in this pilgrim way,
Leaning on the everlasting arms.

While we sing, we know better. We know what these governors did not know and could not know. We know that there can be no "safe and secure" in the modes of fear or coercion or hate. The only route to "safe and secure" is a hope beyond the vagaries of the historical process. And while we may, together, voice such a hope, we are not immune from these historical vagaries. Thus the vagaries of genocide and slavery linger as we face our common life; we are not, in our bold singing, immune from their residue. Thus every time the church meets, we celebrate the long deep hope while at the same time we acknowledge the world in front of us with honesty. That world in front of us does not consist in only the long line of noble presidents (or kings) or in wars endlessly fought and won. Rather, it consists in the long-running narratives of hurt and hope. Good history will include a recital of all those who hurt and those who cause hurt, of those who hope and those who refuse hope and end in the menace of despair.

Our talk about the Holy One as "the Lord of history" is to infer that our human efforts at management and control are always at best penultimate. This is a reality that is very hard for governors to understand and compute. But the church knows that truth quite readily. That is why we sing hymns of praise to the one who ultimately governs the life of the world and our lives. That is why, moreover, the governor gets only one line in the creed: "Crucified under Pontius Pilate." The rest of that paragraph in the creed shows that the forceful effort of the Roman governor was futile. He could not keep his domain "safe and secure" from all the alarms evoked by Jesus. His domain was open to the power of hurt and to the work of the Holy One. While the church knows this, governors always learn it a bit late.

5

ESSENTIAL COMPONENTS OF A GOVERNMENT?

THIS REFLECTION HAS been triggered by a remarkable statement by Paul Krugman, "Blackmailers without a Cause," *New York Times* (February 3, 2023). I will come to that later. Krugman's phrasing has caused me to think about what is required for the formation of a workable government. These requirements can range from the simplest arrangements to the most complex structures of administration, depending on how "hands off" or "hands on" a government might tend to be. The more authoritarian a government, the more it may intrude into every facet of common life.

It will not surprise you that I thought first of the emergence of government in the Old Testament. The evidence we have of early tribal Israel suggests a simple, informal governance by elders. The book of Judges, moreover, attests to sporadic military heroes who came to exercise great and durable influence. Clearly, tribal structures had no need for, and no doubt refused and resisted, any more elaborate governmental ordering. With the emergence of the state under Saul, David, and Solomon, matters became more complex. The recurring staples in this period of emergence of the state consist in *military leaders* and *priests*, that is, a concern for *power* and the *symbols of legitimacy*.

The biblical text provides a quick summary of David's governmental ordering:

> *So David reigned over all Israel; and David administered justice and equity to all his people. Joab son of Zeruiah was over the army; Jehoshaphat son of Ahilud was recorder; Zadok son of Ahitub and Ahimelech son of Abiathar were*

> *priests; Seriah was secretary; Benaiah son of Jehoiada was over the Cherethites and the Pelethites; and David's sons were priests. (2 Sam 8:15–18)*

In addition to a military leader (Joab son of Zeruiah) who figures prominently in David's narrative, and priests (Zadok and Ahimelech plus "David's sons"), the governmental roster includes a recorder (*mazkir*), Jehoshaphat son of Ahilud, and a secretary (*sopher),* Seriah. It is evident that a movement toward centralized government also eventuated in a move toward written records as the oral culture of tribal Israel was left behind. A state must have a long memory, not only of property arrangements, but also of court decisions ("justice and equity"), and memory of debts and offenses against the public order. No doubt David's "recorder" and "secretary" were kept busy preserving the memory of the state. We may imagine that what the recorder and secretary wrote down was the beginning of "state secrets" and "classified documents" that have belatedly come to be taken as the "crown jewels" of the "intelligence community." If one were a vulnerable subsistence peasant, one would at all costs avoid being "written down" or "written up." Thus David Graeber, *Debt: The First 5000 Years,* observes that peasant revolts throughout history always have as a high priority the intent to burn official records that are essentially records of debt. King David evidently was not very far along in this process, but a beginning has been made.

It is noteworthy that David is here credited with doing "justice and equity" (v. 15; *mispat, sedeqah*). We are not told more of this, but we notice early on that David attracted those who are in distress, debt, and discontent (1 Sam 22:2). Perhaps it was hoped that he would administer some economic redress. He is remembered as being in uncommon solidarity with his people (2 Sam 23:13–17). The phrasing of this word pair in verse 15 is readily reiterated in the "royal" Psalm 72:

> *Give the king your* justice, *O God,*
> *and your* righteousness *to a king's son. (Ps 72:1)*

David's rebel son, Absalom, is remembered as an administrator of economic justice (2 Sam 15:1–6). In this Absalom has little in common with his acquisitive half-brother Solomon.

We are able to see, in the case of Solomon, that a more highly developed officialdom was on its way, in contrast to the simpler order of David (see 2 Kings 4:1–6). Solomon's government is a bit more complex. There are, of necessity, some recurring features. The roster of officials includes a son of Zadok as *priest*, and then in traditional fashion lists David's *two priests*, Zadok and Abiathar. This list apparently has forgotten that already in 1 Kings 2:26–27 Solomon has purged Abiathar from his court. Benaiah continues as *army commander*, while Joab disappears from the roster (see 1 Kings 2:28–35). Jehoshaphat continues as recorder (*mazkir*) after David. Two new secretaries (*sopherim*) are named. But what most interest us are the innovations with the last four names that have no counterpart in David's list:

- Azariah is "over the officials," perhaps suggesting a more expansive bureaucracy that required oversight;
- Zabud as the "king's friend." The phrase is unclear to us. Perhaps it is nothing more than a special personal friend of the king; or perhaps it is an identifiable government role as a "roving ambassador" to look after the king's interest and intent. We may surmise that David had many friends whereas Solomon needed to have one designated.
- Ahishar is in charge of "the house," suggesting more royal property to which to attend.
- Most especially Adoniram was over "forced labor," for which there is nothing comparable with David (see 1 Kings 5:14 as well). Adoram (likely the same as Adoniram in 1 Kings 12:18) must have represented what was most resented and resisted by the populace, who comes to a sorry end through the violence of a popular uprising (1 Kings 12:18).

Thus on all counts Solomon's government is more expansive and more complex than that of David, much more a regulation of ambitious rules with an acquisitive intent. It is worth noting that there is here no mention of "justice and righteousness" as with David, perhaps suggesting that the old assumptions of covenantalism have now been expelled from the royal horizon. (We may take the phrase in 1 Kings 10:9 as pertains to Solomon as nothing more than conventional court flattery.) Solomon's roster of officials suggests a greater need to exercise control; but then, with his amassing great wealth, Solomon has much more to control than did his father, David. It is to be noted that Solomon's governmental roster is immediately followed in 1 Kings 4:7–19 with a detailed account of the tax-collecting apparatus of Solomon. Clearly his regime cannot be understood apart from a heavy accent on taxation; see 1 Kings 12:1–19. The data on David has no such counterpart.

We may consider, third, that the book of Deuteronomy traces out a model of government that is marked by the covenantal aspects of the Mosaic-tribal tradition. This matter has been well noted by both Norbert Lohfink, "Distribution of the Functions of Power: The Laws Concerning Public Affairs in Deuteronomy 16:18–18:22," and by S. Dean McBride, "Polity of the Covenant People: The Book of Deuteronomy," in *The Song of Power and the Power of Song: Essays on the Book of Deuteronomy*, edited by Duane Christensen (Winona Lake, IN: Eisenbrauns, 1993), 336–52, and 62–77. Lohfink works backward from the political theory of Montesquieu concerning the separation of powers for the maintenance of a viable government. Thus in these chapters of the Book of Deuteronomy we get this plot of organization:

- municipal judges (16:18–20);
- judicial procedures (17:2–7);
- a court of appeals (17:8–13);
- a king with circumscribed powers (17:14–20);
- priests and Levites (18:1–8); and
- a prophetic office (18:15–22).

This roster identifies all of the ingredients essential to a government. Each office, moreover, is restrained by the claims and limits of covenantal righteousness. As Lohfink has seen, such limitations preclude any excessive accumulation of power or wealth, especially of the kind subsequently modeled and embodied by Solomon (and in the case of Lohfink as a Jesuit, the imperial Vatican). Thus the Deuteronomic model of public power directly joins issue with the near-absolutism of royal power as it was exercised in the Davidic dynasty. The contrast between *local covenantal authority* and *unrestrained royal power* is stark and compelling. The matter of "checks and balances" is old and long running. One mantra of resistance to royal absolutism, twice voiced in the tradition, goes like this:

> *We have no portion in David,*
> *no share in the son of Jesse!*
> *Everyone to your tents, O Israel.*

This mantra is voiced in 2 Samuel 20:1 by a Benjaminite, Bichri, who resists the assertion of David's power. It is reiterated in 1 Kings 12:16 in a refusal of the heavy taxation proposed by Rehoboam over the Northern tribes. It requires no great imagination to see that in our current political scene such sentiments are revoiced and reperformed by protest groups, sometimes violently. Such protests often have no positive political agenda, but only resist and refuse what is perceived to be, as in older days, excessive concentration of power that is inevitably oppressive and exploitative.

The models of David (2 Sam 8:15–18), Solomon (1 Kings 4:1–6, 7–19), and Deuteronomy (16:18–18:22) exhibit various efforts to identify and install what is required for the sake of governance. By comparing and contrasting these several models we can see how differences emerge, depending on the simplicity or complexity of governance, depending on the delicate balance of power between governors and governed, and depending on the coercion required for the sake of revenue.

With this biblical retrospect, I turn now to the remarkable observation of Paul Krugman to which I have alluded. Krugman has observed that for all of the posturing of Republicans concerning "cutting the budget," in fact they have no actual proposal in hand for it. They have, moreover, little energy for such work beyond lip service, preferring to engage in the relatively cost-free exercise of culture war. Krugman sees most clearly that in fact there is very little to be cut from the federal budget because the budget is largely divided among four expenditures: the military, Social Security, Medicare, and Medicaid. Krugman's stunning conclusion is this:

> *As always the fundamental fact about the budget is that the federal government is basically an insurance company with an army.*

The "insurance company" of the federal budget includes Social Security, Medicare, and Medicaid. The "army" is the extensive, expansive military establishment. For political reasons, no serious cuts will be made in any of these expenditures. The GOP does not ever want to cut the military budget. And cutting the "insurance" programs is politically unthinkable. So no cuts! Krugman judges that the MAGA Republicans are "rich in nihilism." He avers,

> *It's dangerous when a political party is willing to burn things down unless it gets its way; it's even more dangerous when that party just wants to watch things burn.*

For our topic of governance, what interests us is Krugman's wise listing of the essentials of government as "army" and "insurance company." There are, to be sure, many other features and functions of government, but they do not claim great portions of the federal budget. Thus we may set Krugman's survey alongside the summaries of David, Solomon, and Deuteronomy to see what is essential in governance. It is useful and important to recognize that the present debate about the role of government is part of an ongoing and inescapable discussion, as we adjudicate simplicity and complexity, localism and concentrated power, and the extent to which government is involved in various aspects of our common life. It is elementally the case that for all the posturing about "small government," the truth is that all such serious public matters (health, housing, education, and defense) the involvement of the government is essential and indispensable. The little note on David concerning "justice and equity" (2 Sam 8:15) is a clue to how we in the church may think, speak, and act about governance. We may be sure that there is no government initiative in which matters of justice and righteousness are not at stake. We know, moreover, that justice and righteousness depend, in covenantal-prophetic tradition, on identifying the most vulnerable neighbors among us, and finding ways to include them in the management and benefits of good governance. Amid the nihilism of the MAGA crowd, we have opportunity to think clearly about matters of taxation and the distribution of resources. When we adjudicate the matter in the presence of the most vulnerable, we will come soon enough to consider reparations for the most severely "left behind."

The church's role, signaled by "priests" in the roster of David and Solomon, and by "priests" and "prophets" in Deuteronomy, is to keep front and center the issue of justice and "righteousness toward our most vulnerable neighbors. Such a role allows for the church's generous practice of charity; but it runs well beyond charity to policy. It is the work of the church to care vigorously about justice and righteousness in policy. Among other things, that must surely mean the maintenance and extension of Krugman's "insurance" to the most vulnerable.

One other thought. Both the rosters of David and Solomon include among essential officers "scribes" (*sopherim*) and "recorders" (*mazkirim*). That is, governance is a "writing thing." That is why we currently have such demanding engagement about "classified documents." A modest, simple oral society has no need for such writing.

But as soon as government becomes more complex and bureaucratic, it depends on written records, most notably to make recruitment lists, tax lists, and records of debt. The secretaries and recorders listed in these rosters are elsewhere designated as "scribes." Scribes were the ones with a learned capacity for writing, recording, and remembering. It is this characterization that leads me, amid a reflection on government, to the singular words assigned to Jesus in the Gospel of Matthew that occur nowhere else in Gospel memory:

> *Therefore every scribe who has been trained for the kingdom of heaven is like the master of a household who brings out of his treasure what is new and what is old. (Matt 13:52)*

The new government of the coming regime of God will require scribes who are skilled recorders, rememberers, and interpreters of the tradition. Such scribes, in this perspective, have a special capacity (a) to bring out from the tradition what is new, and (b) to bring out of the tradition what is old. The scribe is to engage the tradition, the lively memory of the community, in order to *recall the old lessons learned*, but to be able, at the same time, to *offer fresh interpretation* that may permit and authorize society (and government) to open new vistas of well-being.

It occurs to me that amid the pressure and demands of Krugman's "army and insurance company," social well-being depends on skilled interpreters of the tradition who know how to value what is done and settled, and to know, at the same time, how to open the tradition to new initiatives for the sake of well-being. It may indeed be the religious community—Jews, Christians, and Muslims—that has the capacity and the responsibility to handle our societal traditions in generative ways. Without such work we are likely to reiterate old errors or, alternatively, to become unmoored in innovation. There is good reason that much of the church, through its history, has been committed to a "learned ministry," to a ministry capable of and prepared for critical study of and reflection on our social past. King Solomon embodies the unknowing dismissal of the past, as he eliminated Abiathar, priest of the old tradition. It is for this reason that Jeremiah instructs his community, in its belated days,

> *Stand at the crossroads, and look,*
> *and ask for the ancient paths,*
> *where the good way lies; and walk in it,*
> *and find rest for your souls. (Jer 6:16)*

Old paths of Torah are the paths of neighborliness. The community, in its amnesia and its radical new modes, requires the ballast of such critical remembering. Religious leaders are peculiarly situated precisely for such work.

8

RESCINDING ABSOLUTES

THE "DOCTRINE OF Discovery" is a papal bull issued by Pope Alexander VI in 1493, one year after Columbus's "big discovery." Entitled *Inter caetera*, the papal edict gave Spain (and subsequently other European powers) free rein and complete access to the "New World" with a right to its natural resources (gold!) and with authorization to convert, enslave, or kill the indigenous populations.* Forerunners to this papal declaration were *Dum diversus* in 1452 and *Romanus Pontifex*, both by Pope Nicholas V, in 1452 and 1455. Thus the Vatican had a longstanding interest in the authorization of colonization completed in 1493. The doctrine reflected the assumed superiority and entitlement of white Europeans to indigenous populations, and authorized wholesale violence against the "new land," its resource, and its populations. It was a declaration that opened the door to complete exploitation of the "new world" by the "old powers" of Europe. The doctrine was, moreover, incorporated into US law by the US Supreme Court and Chief Justice John Marshall in 1823, which would serve well the aggressive violence of President Andrew Jackson against native peoples.

It is easy enough to see that the doctrine served to advance the ideological claims and interests of white, Western male power. That

---

* The most accessible discussion of the papal encyclical known to me is a special edition of *Intotemak*, a study of Indigenous relations by the Mennonite Church of Canada: Cheryl Woelk and Steve Heinrichs, eds., *Yours, Mine, Ours: Unraveling the Doctrine of Discovery* (Winnipeg, MB: Mennonite Church Canada, 2016). In the issue, see especially Robert L. Miller, "The International Law of Colonialism," 21–27.

ideology, moreover, has persisted and has been variously utilized to justify much US foreign policy, including the guise of "the white man's burden" and eventually "the Manifest Destiny" of the United States with its readiness to intrude on and invade other nation states according to our perceived national interest, from the Halls of Montezuma to the shores of Tripoli. That ideology has gone, for the most part, unquestioned in the councils of policy makers, though there has been a long-running protest against the doctrine among indigenous peoples and their allies. Clearly the ideology continues to flourish among us, with its most recent expression in the broadly based assault against LGBTQ persons in our society. It is all of a piece!

There has been, to be sure, a long advocacy among indigenous peoples to have the doctrine revoked. It was not, however, until March 30, 2023, that the Vatican finally took the action to repudiate the doctrine and its inherent violence. In a reversal of its own "infallibility," the Vatican in its repudiation declared,

> *It [the Vatican for the church] renounces the mindset of cultural or racial superiority which allowed for that objectification or subjection of people, and strongly condemns any attitudes or actions that threaten or damage the dignity of the human person. . . . The Vatican's nullification was too late to stop the destructive impact of colonialization, as European expansion was fueled by a sort of missionary sense the Western monarchies had a right to go these new lands and to take from them the resources and if necessary to put down people, including enslaving them. (Rev. David McCallum, executive director of the Program for Discerning Leadership in Rome)*

The cry against this doctrine has revolved around the tag phrase "Rescind the doctrine." The long-running outcry against the doctrine is based on the insistence that such a brutal immorality as the doctrine must fully give way to the reality of human suffering and human possibility. The ground for refusing rescinding this claim has been the assertion that such claims by the church are immutable and must be kept in place. But of course the reality is that all such "absolutes" are historically conditioned and are filtered through the vested interest and the gains to be made for the people who control the processes of decree making. It turns out, through the repudiation of the doctrine by Pope Francis, that no absolute that stands against human dignity and human well-being is a sustainable absolute. All such claims are relative to time, place, circumstance, and vested interest. Thus the repudiation by the pope is a recognition that no such ideological claim can stand against the will of the creator for human well-being.

This action by Pope Francis set me to thinking about the revocation of absolutes. The phrase captures the irony of an illusion. The phrase requires us to see that our most cherished absolutes are readily seen to be less than absolute. Indeed, it may be suggested that our present so-called culture wars in our society are conflicts and adjudications concerning old absolutes that are widely seen to less than absolute. Thus many so-called conservatives are advocates for old absolutes, including white male superiority. The opponents of such absolutes operate on the assumption that all such old ideological claims are less than absolute, and can and must be modified for the sake human flourishing. Specifically, the brazen assault on the rights and well-being of LBGTQ persons is an unmistakable example of defending old absolutes of white hetero-sexual privilege and preference, an old absolute that in the long run will not stand because it is morally reprehensible, and denies protection to the most vulnerable among us. Thus the work is to show that all such old absolutes are flawed and ideologically tilted in a way that musts be seen for what it is.

As I thought further on this matter of repudiating absolutes, it occurred to me that as we age and mature, we often have awareness of the absolutes of our childhood given us by authority figures (parents, teachers) that we have readily accepted as absolute. The process of maturation, among other things, is a process of recognizing such long-standing absolutes are all too often ideological imports that in our maturity must be repudiated. Thus "father knows best" or "teacher said" (or any such formulation) is a clue to ideological formulation. And of course it is no less so for the claims imposed through the privilege of class, race, or gender. For all of us the work is to attend to social reality with reference to pain and to test every absolute in terms of the pain it may cause or the pain it may alleviate. Thus I suggest that every absolute that causes or condones human suffering cannot stand. It is for that reason that a lively faith must include a "culture of interpretation" that is tirelessly at work in an appropriation of the past that is critically informed. When the past is embraced without critical awareness, hurtful ideological claims are sure to follow.

As I write these lines, I have at my elbow the words of challenge addressed in poetic formulation to a company of displaced people:

> *Do not remember the former things,*
> *or consider the things of old.*
> *I am about to do a new thing;*
> *now it springs forth, do you not perceive it? (Isa 43:18–19)*

The poet addressed a community of faith that delighted, in its displacement, to reiterate old faith claims, most importantly, a memory of the exodus event. The poet, to the contrary, wants to insist on attention to present historical reality in which "a new thing" is happening. The new thing, in the book of Isaiah, is a new exodus of God's people to be wrought by appeal, to the Persians under the leadership of Cyrus, who is recognized as a messiah (Isa 45:1). Of course it requires a certain perspective to be able to see the defeat of Babylon by Persia as a new exodus for Israel. But that is exactly the point! That perspective is one that affirms that YHWH, the Lord of the exodus, continues to do emancipatory work in the world for powerless people. That perspective permits us to see that the God of emancipation is not "back here" in the book of Exodus, but here and now present doing emancipatory work. A move beyond the "old absolute" of the exodus memory permitted the poet to perceive his own time and place as one occupied by God's liberating presence and purpose. It is particularly from 2 Isaiah that we get testimony to the God who creates newness, who makes possible a way out of no way.

This accent by Isaiah on newness amid displacement is echoed by the prophet Jeremiah. In the exile Israel could readily remember the old covenant of Sinai. In the face of that old memory Jeremiah could declare God's new covenant that is grounded in God's ready forgiveness:

> *No longer shall they teach one another, or say to each other, "Know the Lord," for they shall all know me, from the least of them to the greatest, says the Lord; for I will forgive their iniquity and remember their sin no more. (Jer 31:34)*

And while the phrase *new covenant* was readily appropriated by the early church, there is nothing "supersessionist" about it, for the God of Moses is endlessly making new covenants. In like manner Ezekiel can anticipate a "new temple" that will be perfectly symmetrical, from which the glory of the Lord will not depart (Ezek 40–48):

> *This gate shall remain shut; it shall not be opened, and no one shall enter by it; for the Lord, the God of Israel, has entered by it; therefore it shall remain shut. (44:2)*

Along with the "new temple," Ezekiel can anticipate a new people propelled by a new spirit:

> *Cast away from you all the transgressions that you have committed against me, and get yourself a new heart and a new spirit! (18:31)*

> *A new heart I will give you, and a new spirit I will put within you; and I will remove from your body the heart of stone and give you a heart of flesh. (36:26)*

Israel is endlessly summoned from its old absolutes to the newness God is doing among them. And of course the new regime that Jesus proclaimed as "the kingdom of God" is a summons to new discipleship and new obedience, a summons that mandates departure from old "absolutes. Thus we may formulate a rule of prophetic thinking:

> *Occasions of displacement and disorientation both require and permit the formulation and embrace of new promises and new responsibilities.*

Or as the poet James Russell Lowell has it,

> *New occasions teach new duties,*
> *time makes ancient good uncouth.*
>
> *"The Present Crisis," 1845*

It turns out that the repudiation of *Inter caetera* by Pope Francis is fully congruent with the new-making God who is always calling us out beyond old settlements to new possibilities and new demanding obediences. The church is in witness-bearing community to the newness God is doing among us. It is of course possible for the church to wallow in its old absolutes. That, however, is not required. It is also possible for us to notice newness, even when it pushes against our settled treasured comfort zones.

> *Your word is a lamp to my feet*
> *and a light to my path. (Ps 119:105)*

7

THE STRANGE WORK OF SONS-IN-LAW

IN HER BOOK *Strongmen: From Mussolini to the Present* (W. W. Norton, 2020), Ruth Ben-Ghiat considers the roster of "strongmen" who have dominated much of the world stage in recent time. Her scholarly expertise is in Italian fascism and the career of Mussolini. In this book, however, she considers a range of strongmen after Mussolini, including Silvio Berlusconi in Italy, Viktor Orbán in Hungary, Recep Tayyip Erdoğan in Turkey, Muammar Gaddafi in Libya, Mobutu Sese Seko in Zaire, and Donald Trump in the United States. She traces out the characteristic conditions and practices that recur among strongmen who in various ways have distorted or scuttled democratic realities in their several nation-states. Such men, she shows, are variously marked by corruption, readiness for violence, a craving for money and attention, and sexual predation. Everything about this company concerns the acquisition, expansion, and maintenance of power in the most ruthless ways, before which democratic processes, procedures, and institutions are markedly vulnerable. Most of this data is not new, but it is greatly helpful to have it all on exhibit in her discerning exposition.

It is notable that these strongmen characteristically merge together the control and benefit of their families and the levers of power and access to public money. The distinctions between family and state become vague and trespassable:

> *Strongmen are family men in their own fashion. To block criticism and engage in corrupt practices while minimizing the chance of exposure, they establish inner sanctums composed of family members and trusted cronies. The leader's children*

> *may run the official family business, as with Berlusconi and Trump, or the unofficial family business of money-laundering, which was the case with Mobutu's son Kongulu and many other offspring of autocrats.* (Strongmen, *146)*

But then I was quite taken by surprise with this comment:

> *Sons-in-law also have a prominent role in strongmen governance. Mussolini made his son-in-law Galeazzo Ciano foreign minister in 1936, used him as "a tool of his personal politics," and then had Ciano executed for voting in 1943 to remove him from power. Orban's son-in-law Istvan Tiborcz, a business man, has amassed a net worth of over 100 million euros, but the Hungarian government dropped corruption probes initiated by the European Union (EU) against him. Berat Albayrak, accused by multiple foreign governments of illegal activities while serving as Turkish energy minister, is now Erdogan's treasury and finance minister. Jared Kushner, presidential advisor, pursues private Kushner and Trump family financial interests along with his government assignments. (146)*

I had never thought before how these strongmen, with their daughters close at hand and held in the orbit of family power and wealth, depended on the husbands of the daughters as accomplices and placeholders in their practice.

When I read that I thought, as is my wont to do, of two cases in the Old Testament wherein sons-in-law feature in Israel's narrative. The first case concerns David as son-in-law of King Saul. As you know, that relationship did not turn out well, at least not for Saul. The narrative report of their interaction is fast moving. At the outset, after David's astonishing defeat of the Philistine giant, Saul asks his general, Abner, about the identity of David:

Abner, whose son is this young man? (1 Sam 17:55)

Abner does not know. Saul asks directly when Abner brings the young David into the presence of the king:

Whose son are you, young man? (v. 58)

David answers Saul discreetly and directly:

I am the son of your servant Jesse the Bethlehemite. (v. 58)

Two things then happen quickly. First Saul's son, Jonathan, the crown prince, is smitten with David (1 Sam 18:1–4). And David was remarkably successful in battle, so much so that Saul in his jealousy wanted to kill him (vv. 5–10). It has taken only eleven verses from David's introduction to Saul to Saul's lethal resentment of him. But David eludes him, as he will continue to do in the extended narrative. Then Saul tries a very different tactic. He seeks to marry his daughter, Merah, to David, expecting David to be his great warrior who may in turn be killed by the Philistines (vv. 17–19). When the effort with Merab fails, Saul designates his other daughter, Michal, to be David's bride. Saul's intent for David is nefarious:

Let me give her to him that she may be a snare for him and
that the hand of the Philistines may be against him. (v. 21)

And so we get a report on David's new status as son-in-law of the king:

Saul commanded his servants, "Speak to David in private
and say, 'See, the king is delighted with you, and all his
servants love you; now then, become the king's son-in-law.'"
So Saul's servants reported these words to David in private.
And David said, "Does it seem to you a little thing to become

> *the king's son-in-law, seeing that I am a poor man and of no repute?" (vv. 22–23)*

Saul sets for David a demanding, dangerous bride price of a hundred foreskins of Philistine warriors, a requirement sure to get David killed by the Philistines. Again Saul is foiled, as David successfully meets Saul's quota of Philistine foreskins and so qualifies for the marriage to the king's daughter (v. 27). So the couple is married. Saul has his son-in-law!

Thus the vexed competitive relationship is established and the issue is joined. The contest for kingship is between father-in-law and son-in-law. In what follows Saul tries repeatedly to kill David. David, in response, has more reason to wish Saul dead, but restrains himself. At the end of the struggle between the two, David acquits himself with grace and dignity as he eventually laments the death of his friend Jonathan and his father-in-law, Saul, in most elegant terms. In his lament, Saul is mentioned twice, Jonathan four times:

> *You mountains of Gilboa,*
> *let there be no dew or rain upon you,*
> *nor bounteous fields!*
> *For there the shield of the mighty was defiled,*
> *the shield of Saul, anointed with oil no more.*
> *From the blood of the slain,*
> *from the fat of the mighty,*
> *the bow of Jonathan did not turn back,*
> *nor the sword of Saul return empty.*
> *Saul and Jonathan, beloved and lovely!*
> *In life and in death they were not divided;*
> *they were swifter than eagles,*
> *they were stronger than lions. . . .*
> *How the mighty have fallen*
> *in the midst of the battle!*

Jonathan lies slain upon your high places.
I am distressed for you, my brother Jonathan;
greatly beloved were you to me;
your love to me was wonderful,
passing the love of women.
How the mighty have fallen,
and the weapons of war perished! (2 Sam 1:21–27)

This relationship of father-in-law and son-in-law was deeply complex. Indeed, the relationship had no chance of success because David, according to the narrator, was destined by his secret anointing to become king (1 Sam 16:13). That secret anointing was no part of Saul's reckoning, and so the uneven contest between the two turned out in the only way it could, with Saul's death and David's subsequent triumph. The complexity of *a public power contest* and *a familial conflict* is about what we might expect when a son-in-law is not content with his subordinate role with reference to a father-in-law who is a "strongman" bent on power.

The other "son-in-law connection" in the Old Testament that comes to mind is the little-noted one concerning Solomon and his sons-in-law. In 1 Kings 4:7–19, it is reported that Solomon had created twelve tax officials to preside over twelve tax districts in order to raise revenue for the opulent extravagance of the royal court. The number twelve matches the months of the year, as each tax district had to underwrite one month of the royal expenditure. The tax districts of Solomon, it appears, paid no attention to the old tribal boundaries, but were simply devised for maximum competence and effectiveness in tax collection. The roster of tax officials and tax districts looks quite routine and without much special interest. Except this: in two of the tax districts the tax official was Solomon's son-in-law, each married to a daughter of Solomon:

Benabinadab, in all Naphathdor (he had Taphath, Solomon's daughter, as his wife) . . . Ahimaaz, in Naphtali (he had

> *taken Basemath, Solomon's daughter, as his wife). (1 Kings 4:11, 15)*

Appointment as a tax officer must have been an insider practice. We know nothing of the other tax officials in this list, but it is likely that they were all "political appointments" from well-connected families. The naming of two sons-in-law in this list manifests the way in which family connections were injected into the royal rule of Solomon.

We may hunch that tax collecting in ancient Israel was something of an exploitative practice. The evidence for this, in addition to Solomon's readiness to draft his own subjects into state slavery, is the narrative report in 1 Kings 12:1–19. The narrative reports on tax revolt at the end of Solomon's reign. The tax system (and the tax revolt) exhibit the co-optation of subsistence peasants into the apparatus of the urban elites, who lived from the surplus wealth produced by the peasants.

Solomon, and presumably his daughters, Taphath and Basemath, were particularly indifferent to the plight of the subsistence peasants and regarded them only as a source of coerced wealth. The presence of the two sons-in-law offers evidence of how family and state interests were easily intermingled to the great benefit of the insiders.

It is inescapable in this connection that I would mention Jared Kushner, son-in-law of Donald Trump. Ruth Ben-Ghiat has already shown how Trump belongs in the company of the strongmen. The operation of Kushner in Trump's White House exhibits the way in which family and state interests were readily intermingled. Public reports make clear that Kushner acquired a great deal of private money from his interactions with the regime of Saudi Arabia, all the while utilizing the levers of state power to promote private interest.

While it may be possible to let the biblical evidence concerning Solomon's two sons-in-law to illumine the Trump-Kushner connection, that is not my intent here. We already know enough about that exploitative connection concerning Trump and his family. Here my interest is to read in the other direction, that is, to let what we know of Trump-Kushner and the other strongmen and their sons-in-law illumine the biblical narrative. Thus the son-in-law connection, noted by Ben-Ghiat, lends itself to understanding the two relationships in the Old Testament I have mentioned. Thus Saul easily comingled family interest and the interest of his partly formed state. The narrative suggests, moreover, that the initiation and interest in the matter was all on Saul's side, with David being a willing participant in the project, perhaps as an opportunist. That is, David was a willing participant in the Saul narrative, thus moving toward his "destiny" as a would-be king. His attitude and conduct are complex and he manipulates the matter with great cleverness, ostensibly respecting his father-in-law, all the while promoting his own very different agenda.

In the case of Solomon, these sparse notes on privileged sons-in-law (who have only twelve seconds of fame) fit with what we know of Solomon and his greedy governance. Solomon is easily revealed as an aggressive, wealth-accumulating, security-seeking ruler who had little interest in the well-being of his subjects, with no regard for subsistence peasants who were reduced to state slavery (1 Kings 5:13). We have no reason to think that his two daughters or his two sons-in-law in any way dissented from his predatory practice. Rather, it is likely that they were willing and docile recipients of the benefits of such governance.

We may judge then, with the two footnotes concerning family engagement, that the temple in Jerusalem was built by Solomon as a monument to the wealth and power of a strongman. It is ironic that the temple is linked to a strongman. But we have long had good reason to conclude that the temple was an ill-suited vehicle for Israel's covenantal faith. Indeed, it is reported that already at the dedication of Solomon's temple his grand edifice could not ever contain the reach of the holy God (2 Kings 8:27). The presence of the two sons-in-law in the official roster simply confirms the uneasy ambiguity of faith and power under the aegis of Solomon.

In the case of Saul and David, David manages, by the skin of his teeth, to come off as innocent; he is nonetheless willing to engage, as son-in-law, in the power-seeking of Saul. There are no innocents in the overlap of state and family.

We may finish our reflection on this recurring interface of family and state with the utterances of Jesus concerning the presence of family in his coming regime. In his teaching Jesus makes clear the radicality of his coming governance that does not expect family matters to intrude on the coming regime:

> *For I have come to set a man against his father,*
> *and a daughter against her mother,*
> *and a daughter-in-law against her mother-in law;*
> *and one's foes will be members of one's own household.*
> *(Matt 10:35–36)*

Nothing cozy or familial in this governance! And in narrative form, Jesus responds, when told of the arrival of his mother and brothers and sisters,

> *"Who are my mother and my brothers?" And looking at those who sat around him, he said, "Here are my mother and my brothers! Whoever does the will of God is my brother and sister and mother." (Mark 3:32–35)*

Jesus attested that those who are his "kin" are those already engaged in the coming rule of God. This connection reaches beyond self-interest, a reach out of reach of the strongmen and their sons-in-law.

8

ORIGINALISM

I WAS MINDING my own business, reading *Seduced by Story: The Use and Abuse of Narrative*, by Peter Brooks (New York Review Books, 2022). Brooks has spent his distinguished lifetime as a literary critic who pays great attention to the cruciality of narrative as a governing literary genre. In this book he explores the way in which "story" is an open-ended process of interaction between teller and listener, with a playful capacity for the offer of new reality in the generative process between teller and listener. Then, abruptly, I am at page 137. On that page Brooks offers a telling comment on the Supreme Court and its engagement with the Constitution. He takes up the matter because the Constitution itself amounts to something of a narrative reading of reality that invites playful interaction for teller and listener. Brooks comments in particular on the statement of Justice William Brennan, who dissented from the majority opinion in *Michael H. v Gerald D.*

> *The document [the majority ruling] that the plurality construes today is unfamiliar to me. It is not the living charter that I have taken to be our Constitution; it is instead a stagnant, archaic hidebound document steeped in the prejudices and superstitions of a time long past. (137)*

Brennan's assertion, albeit with a critical tilt, identified two views of the US Constitution:

> *a living charter; a stagnant, archaic hidebound document steeped in the prejudices and superstitions of a time long past.*

Brennan observes that the latter view, termed "originalism," has won the day; Brooks writes that originalism has come to fully dominate the horizon of the court. Originalism is the tricky, doubtful claim that the Constitution must adhere to the "original intent" of its framers. But of course such a claim is largely ideology, given the recent ruling of the court on the Second Amendment that surely reached well beyond original intent; moreover, in according the election of 2000 to George W. Bush, the court violated its own presumed adherence to "states rights" and overruling the claims of the State of Florida.

In any case Brooks's quote of Justice Brennan got me thinking about originalism. I am not a student of the Constitution, so will do no more than notice how problematic is the claim for its application to the Constitution and how ideology-laden is the practice of originalism, regardless of its theory.

My interest, as you might expect, is the matter of "originalism" in biblical interpretation. We have long been witness to two forms of biblical originalism, first that of fundamentalism, which focuses on the "red letter" utterances of Jesus, and, second, that of historical-critical attempts to get back to the "original" meaning of the text. Both efforts are ideology laden, either critical study propelled by evolutionism pursued by liberals or the red-letter fundamentalism that most often travels with conservatism. My interest here is to consider briefly the matter of dynamism in the text and in interpretation that undermines any claim of "originalism," as though we might recover the original intent of any of its authors.

We may begin with the prescient work of Gerhard von Rad, in his *Studies in Deuteronomy* (1948, and then in English in with SCM in 1953). In this book von Rad saw the profound tension been the legal-theological material of the Covenant Code and that of the Deuteronomic tradition. He observed that the "laws" in the Covenant Code were given as God's own words, thus investing them with special authority, whereas Deuteronomy is filled with the sermonic flourishes of Moses that include motivational and interpretive commentary along the way:

> *For actually, the most elementary difference between the Book of the Covenant and Deuteronomy—a difference that is particularly striking because the two books do contain so much common material—lies in the fact that Deuteronomy is not divine law in a codified form, but preaching about the commandments—at least, the commandments appear in a form where they are very much interspersed with parenesis. (15)*

Unlike the other legal collections Deuteronomy exhibits, the perfect freedom with which it handles the old traditions and intersperses them with homiletics is something completely new compared with the Book of the Covenant (24). In the Bible itself we may observe the tension between "originalism" of "God's own words" and the freedom of interpretation and commentary that make it possible to rearticulate the text in response to the present social reality of the interpreter. It is the tradition of Deuteronomy, as von Rad has repeatedly shown, that can most self-consciously depart from any originalism, a tradition of interpretive freedom that eventuates in the prophets, the Judaism of Ezra, and the Jesus movement. In the latter case,

> *you have heard it said of old . . . but I say unto you. . . . (Matt 5:27–28)*

We may usefully consider the important tension in the text itself concerning originalism and interpretive freedom, even as the same tension persists in our ongoing work in interpreting the Bible. If we were to adhere to originalism, we might especially appeal to the high theological claim made for Jesus Christ in the Epistle to the Hebrews:

> *Jesus Christ is the same yesterday and today and forever. (Heb 13:8)*

This verse serves to assure Christians under duress that the substance of gospel faith is constant, reliable, and not subject to whims of change.

We might expect that such a claim of constancy would produce an originalist text that would stand firm with compelling and conclusive authority. It turns out, however, that exactly the opposite is the case. The case for the One "begotten not made who is of one substance with the Father" in his hiddenness has evoked and required an endless flow of texts, from the earliest apostle to the Gospel writers and then to centuries of pastors, teachers, poets, scholars, and songwriters, each of whom seeks to articulate the identity of the One who is "the same" in fresh perspective. The juggling act conducted among the Gospel writers makes clear that there can be no single originalist text concerning Jesus, but only many alternative variations, none of which has a claim to closure or privilege.

In seeking what may be originalist about the God of Israel, we might do better to consider the way in which YHWH, as governor, differs from rivals and competitors. The clearest case may be Daniel's confrontation with King Darius who signed an interdict against Daniel. Darius did as his advisors urged:

> *Now, O king, establish the interdict and sign the document,*
> *so that it cannot be changed, according to the law of the*
> *Medes and the Persians, which cannot be revoked. (Dan 6:8)*

The king agrees with his advisors in the narrative and signed the interdict:

> *The thing stands fast, according to the law of the Medes and*
> *Persians, which cannot be revoked. (Dan 6:12)*

This is grim originalism! The matter is made public and cannot be altered. The gods of the Medes and Persians assured an unchanging, unchangeable decree that will determine human outcomes.

Except that YHWH, the God of Israel, wills and acts otherwise:

> *My God sent his angel and shut the lions' mouths so that they would not hurt me, because I was found blameless before him; and also before you, O king, I have done no wrong.* (Dan 6:22)

The God of Israel changes what cannot be changed! Unlike the gods of the Medes and the Persians, the God of Israel is master of every originalism, and can act in freedom. It is no wonder that King Darius breaks out in doxology to the God of Israel who breaks open what the other gods had patently tried to close off. Darius seems relieved to have an alternative to his own gods of changelessness:

> *For he is the living God,*
> *enduring forever.*
> *His kingdom shall never be destroyed,*
> *and his dominion has no end.*
> *He delivers and rescues,*
> *he works signs and wonders in heaven and on earth;*
> *for he has saved Daniel*
> *from the power of the lions.* (Dan 6:26–27)

Thus we might expect, in biblical testimony, that the emergence (or eruption) of new possibility could be the order of the day. In that case no text can remain unchallenged in its claim, because this God works newness beyond old formulation. Consider these cases in point:

In the flood narrative of Genesis 6–9, nothing is changed about the human condition by the flood. The "imagination of the human heart" is as evil after the flood (Gen 8:21) as it was before (Gen 6:5). What has changed is the resolve of God to destroy or in turn to rehabilitate. God, in response to circumstance, will not stay locked in to old textual formulations.

- In Hosea 11:5–7, the God of Israel in anger prepared to have Israel devoured by the sword. But then, in verses 8–9, God abruptly changes direction as though the God of Israel had a moment of fresh self-reflection:

How can I give you up, Ephraim?
How can I hand you over, O Israel?
How can I make you like Admah?
How can I treat you like Zeboiim?
My heart recoils within me;
my compassion grows warm and tender.
I will not execute my fierce anger;
I will not again destroy Ephraim;
for I am God and no mortal,
the Holy One in your midst,
and I will not come in wrath. (Hos 11:8–9)

This God is not and will not be trapped in old formulation, even if formulations are of God's own making.

- In Jeremiah 18:7, God may decree against a nation that it will be plucked up and broken down. Such a decree, however, is not like that of the Medes and the Persians—fixed, permanent, and beyond recall. Rather, the future of the formula is governed by an "if" of conditionality:

If that nation, concerning which I have spoken, turns from its evil, I will change my mind about the disaster that I intend to bring on it. (Jer 18:8)

God is free to change God's mind, to redirect attention, and to issue a fresh decree of planting and building. The world is not fated, because the creator God remains free in the exercise of governance. Conversely, a positive decree can and will be revoked if circumstance requires cancellation of the good God had intended to do (Jer 18:10).

- Most familiarly, the poet in the exile can have God move past "old things" for the newness of rescue and homecoming:

Do not remember the former things,
or consider the things of old.
I am about to do a new thing;
now it springs forth, do you not perceive it? (Isa 43:18–19)

This God is no prisoner of past utterance. This God will not be held in hock to previous utterance or to ancient text. There can be no originalism wherein an old text can claim continuing unfettered authority.

Robert Alter has nicely written that Judaism is a "culture of interpretation," so that a primary, defining enterprise of Judaism is the continual, open-ended offer of interpretation by many voices from many perspectives, each of which claims attention and consideration. The same culture of interpretation persists in the Christian tradition, though certainly with less freedom and imagination. It remains for Christian practice to learn more fully from Judaism the capacity for such bold, endless interpretation.

When we recognize that such multivoiced interpretation is beyond doubt in the Bible, such a realization may indeed help us to consider the character and quality of the US Constitution as well, as a "living charter" that aims to protect human rights and human well-being with an ever expansive scope. After all, we may well recognize that almost all of our various "stopping places" of drawing a line against new interpretation are most often acts of vested interest. Justice Thomas, an eager advocate for originalism, is willing to roll back constitutional rights for gays and, eventually, for woman as well. But he will stop short concerning rights for nonwhites. If there were no such stopping places in the enterprise of interpretation, we would finally arrive back at the claim that only white male plantation owners really have any rights. I do not know anyone willing (yet!) to go back that far!

I hope it is clear that women and men of faith have a deep reason to resist originalism, which wants to halt the ongoing vitality of the Constitution or the Bible. We would do well to recognize that the God of the Bible—and so also the vision of the Constitution—are open-ended to the truth of emancipation and well-being made possible in and through a community of faithfulness that is not governed by fear. The Puritan pastor John Robinson could declare,

> *There is more truth and light to break forth from God's Holy Word.*

It is for that reason that our interpretive work must continue. The God of the Bible does not intend "closure" around any of our favorite interpretations!

Peter Brooks well understands that there is more than one way to tell a story. There are, to be sure, the "normative storytellers" to whom heed must be paid. But new versions keep arising. In the Old Testament, the identifiable moments for the emergence of new tellings have long been designated JEDP, variant ways of telling the story of ancient Israel. The Gospel writers whom we designate as Matthew, Mark, Luke, and John are communities that told the story of Jesus in very different ways. There are many ways to tell the story of God's life in the world; every one of them wants to be heard, but no one gets it fully right. There are many ways to tell the story of human rights in the United States, and no one finally gets to tell that story in a way that denies rights to others that belong to us all. The attempt to freeze a certain telling as normative is most often an act of fear or vested interest. But the force of the plot of the story itself will always insist on its retelling. We can either be agents for such ongoing telling, or among those who seek to repress such retellings. Insofar as the story is true, it will insist on and receive fresh retellings. Neither our fear nor our vested interest will preclude such retellings!

Part III

NEW WORSHIP

Well, I would say my spirituality for the most part, amounts to exegesis. I think my compelling. encounters with God have been through exegesis of the text. What I have discovered is that I'm not very competent or skillful about meditation. But I am a reader of texts and I continue to draw life and energy, summons and forgiveness out of the windows of the text. I think the Psalms are the script for ongoing conversation with God and, as you may know, I spent a huge amount of energy on lament Psalms. I think I have helped the church rediscover the lament Psalms after the church worked hard to get rid of them. What the lament songs do is to legitimate the voice of faith, the voice of Israel. So that our conversation with God is a genuine dialogue and not a one-way address from God to us. So I think those particular lament Psalms have funded a great deal of my own prayer life, and my understanding that this is a God who can be impinged on and impacted and changed by our prayers. And that means that God must be perceived in quite Jewish ways of dialogue, which makes me very nervous when you get the theological categories of omniscience and omnipotence and omnipresence. I think that the dialogic covenant model is defining for me and the Psalms basically express. I love hymns. I think they are the poetic outlining of faith. Because the poetic lets you override all the theological quarrels. I think there's something very Protestant about having to voice your faith that way. So I love congregational singing. I don't have a singing voice, but I make a joyful noise unto the Lord.

9

INTIMACY BEYOND SCHOLASTICISM

MY THEME FOR this comment comes from a question my friend, Conrad Kanagy, posed for me amid his work to narrate my life. He asked about the attitude of my childhood faith toward science. I am glad for his invitation to reflect on the matter.

My childhood faith—led by my mother and presided over by my father-pastor—was a form of "German pietism" that we practiced readily in our community of German-American immigrants. The phrase *German pietism* is so readily misunderstood in terms of "piety" that I will give it some reflective attention. Pietism arose in Germany in the seventeenth century. It was a response to orthodox, scholastic Lutheranism that trafficked in syllogistic reasoning, insisted on doctrinal certitude, and imposed conformity of thought. In resistance against such reductionism, there arose in the seventeenth century in Germany a movement of deep and serious faith (pietism) that refused such doctrinal exactitude and authoritarianism. It placed its emphasis on personal intimate faith and trust in the Lord Jesus. Among the most prominent, most often mentioned leaders of this movement are

- Philipp Jacob Spener (1635–1705),
- August Hermann Franke (1663–1727), and
- Nikolaus Ludwig von Zinzendorf (1700–1760).

The movement came to expression in a variety of forms, most especially among the Moravians, and through John and Charles Wesley, the Methodist movement. The German immigrant community that is my antecedent community also participated in that movement.

In the nineteenth century, pietism continued to have compelling force, not least among the German Evangelicals from which my family derived. In the nineteenth century pietism was made particularly important through the scholarship of Albrecht Ritschl (1822–1889) and Friedrich Schlieremacher (1768–1834). Schlieremacher was directly involved in the shaping of the faith community from which my family came. The pietism of my German forebears was made more complex and eventually more agile because of the Prussian Union of 1817, when the Prussian King Fredrick William III merged the Lutheran and Reformed Churches into a United Church. The pastors who readily embraced that Union were termed "Union men," because they did not want to linger over the theological niceties of either Lutheranism or Calvinism. (My father, in his turn, was indeed a Union man.) The act of the Union precluded doctrinal exactitude in either a Lutheran or a Calvinist mode. Through the leadership of Schlieremacher, the Prussian Union took on a distinctly pastoral casting that vigorously eschewed scholastic exactitude and intellectual conformity.

My own childhood faith was very much a product of that movement, even though the specificities of pietism were not much talked about among us. My simple formulation of my childhood pietism, given me by my parents in their walk more than their talk, is that we may *love the Lord Jesus* in an intimate and direct way, and our energy is to *care for the vulnerable*, that is, in quite practical ways, "to love God and to love neighbor." My own sense of that faith in practice includes the following:

- Our family practiced "daily devotions" every day at suppertime. This consisted in a devotional tract from the denomination that was called "Daily Talk with God." It provided daily guidance and nurture; it included each day a brief Scripture reading, a brief exposition, and a prayer. Sometimes my mother would read the printed prayer; sometimes my father would offer a prayer.

- The *Evangelical Catechism* occupied central attention in my growing up. It is a little blue book of 128 questions and answers that walks the student through the creed in its three articles, the Ten Commandments, and the Lord's Prayer, the staples of Reformation catechisms. It was designed to prepare young teenagers for confirmation into church life. On the catechism see Frederick Trost, *The Evangelical Catechism: A New Translation for the Twenty-First Century* (Pilgrim, 2009) and my own brief commentary, *The Evangelical Catechism Revisited* (Eden, 1972). The faith to which the catechism bears witness is simply put, direct, and intimate. Thus on "creation" (a subject that draws attention concerning "faith and science,") the catechism offers these simple affirmations:

Q15: How does God constantly prove himself to be the Creator?

A: God constantly proves himself to be the Creator by his fatherly providence, whereby he preserves and governs all things.

Q16: What has God done for you?

A: I believe that God has made me and all creatures; that he has given me and still preserves my body and soul, eyes, ears, and all my members, my reason and all my sense, also food and clothing, home and family, and all my possessions.

Q17: What does God still do for you?

A: God daily and abundantly provides me with all the necessaries of life, protects and preserves me from all danger.

Q18: Why does God do this for you?

A: God does all this out of sheer fatherly and divine goodness and mercy, without any merit or worthiness on my part.

We can notice what is generously affirmed. We can also notice what goes without comment, namely, all the claims that might lead to a clash with science. The catechism will have none of that, nor will the tradition of pietism that informs it.

Most notably the catechism concludes with this question:

Q128: What does our communion daily require of us?

In response the suffering love of the Lord Jesus is articulated. And then this:

A: Lord Jesus, for thee I live, for thee I suffer, for thee I die!
Lord Jesus, thine will I be in life and death!
Grant me, O Lord, eternal salvation! Amen.

We can notice the direct address to "Lord Jesu,s" with whom we are judged to be on the most intimate of terms. One can observe in this answer and its intimate language a shunning of all scholastic formulation.

- Perhaps the most compelling evidence of the practice of pietism in my memory is my memory that members of the church would annually stage a major cookout in the fall to make pots of apple butter and applesauce from the fall harvest. The apple produce was then canned and taken to our two "Emmaeus Homes" funded by the church. These "Homes," located in St. Charles and Marthasville, were institutions designed to care for epileptics and "feebleminded" persons. Much of the food for these homes was produced by local congregations, a practice only discontinued when state laws prohibited such food provision. The funding of these homes, along with an orphanage, a hospital, and inner-city Settlement House, constituted a steadfast commitment of the community toward the vulnerable in society. Already in the seventeenth century Franke had founded a school for children and an orphan house funded by his friends. Care for the socially vulnerable was a major mark of the faithful obedience in this tradition.

- The long-running tension between scholastic Lutherans and evangelical pietism in Germany was readily transported to the United States. In the small town where I grew up (and in many similar towns), German immigrants were largely divided into two congregations, one a Missouri Synod Lutheran and the other the evangelical tradition—in my experience, a congregation of the Evangelical Synod. Congregations and pastors of the Missouri Synod were scholastically insistent, whereas the evangelical congregations and pastors were much more attuned to the actual realities of lived life. I can remember that my father, as a pastor, frequently had to adjudicate "mixed marriages" between a Missouri Lutheran and a member of our congregation. The issue most often turned on an authoritarian insistence that made the relationship problematic. It often remained for the evangelical pastor to pick up the pieces of human woundedness from such a relationship. It is striking that we were able to transfer that old German conflict into the American scene.
- The evangelical tradition was characteristically irenic and was most reluctant to engage in doctrinal dispute, being willing and able to allow great latitude in belief and practice. That latitude was made possible (and necessary) by the recognition that human life is bottomlessly complex, and that our grounding is in the grace of God that does not depend on doctrinal exactitude.

All of this background we may take as preliminary and preparatory to our question of faith and science. Perhaps the place to begin with this question is to notice that quite early in the nineteenth century my German evangelical denomination readily embraced "historical criticism" as a legitimate way to study Scripture. The perspective of historical criticism permitted and required consideration of the best scientific learning that we could muster. The Evangelical Union (my church) had a few early skirmishes about the matter, but by the time my father went to seminary (1922) and my brother and I followed him (1954–55), the matter of the critical study of Scripture was a settled matter. Indeed my brother and I were fortunate to have as our Old Testament teacher Allen G. Wehrli (who had been our father's teacher as well), who had studied with Hermann Gunkel at the University of Halle. Wehrli had no hesitation in utilizing the best scientific methods for his teaching.

For the most part we did not notice that in the nineteenth century "critical learning" in Scripture had completely adapted to the evolutionary hypothesis of Darwin and applied it to Scripture. Thus the old "documentary hypothesis" of JEDP was lined out in an evolutionary scheme from the most primitive religion to the most sophisticated. This approach dominated Scripture study until the 1970s. The textbook we read in seminary was *Unraveling the Book of Books* by Ernest Trattner (Kenington, 1929), which was an unapologetic articulation of the evolutionary hypothesis applied to the history of Israelite religion. Further, my father's hero, Harry Emerson Fosdick, a noted "liberal" preaching icon, had published a book articulating the evolutionary hypothesis of how biblical faith "developed."

This tradition of faith did not have a great deal to say about scientific matters. It did affirm, however, that faith must engage with the best learning available, including advances in science. It never saw that emergent science needed in any way to collide with or contradict the claims of faith, because the claims of faith were most passionately cast in personal, interpersonal terms. This casting permitted the tradition to be enormously elastic and agile in its recognition of new learning.

To be sure, the tradition insisted, and continues to insist, that there are compelling moral restraints on the development of scientific learning into technological practice. The criterion for such restraint is of course the damage that such development may cause to the environment and to the most vulnerable of human creatures.

It is the case that such pietism continued much too long in its embrace of a simplistic evolutionary scheme with reference to the Bible and to faith more generally. With the dramatic changes and advances in scientific matters around the developments in quantum physics and the recognition that reality consists in energy as much as substance, the pietistic tradition, like much else for the church, has not adapted as readily as it might. Thus the church, in its pietistic manifestations, is always playing catch-up with new learnings. It is playing catch-up, not because of its resistance but because new learning always requires fresh formulations and articulations of faith. The pietistic tradition has no particular reluctance about such reformulation and articulation.

Just now we may take notice of a new study entitled *Awe: The New Science of Everyday Wonder and How It Can Transform Your Life*, by Dacher Keltner (Penguin, 2023). It is remarkable that such a book is able to label a fresh appreciation of "awe" as "The New Science." Whether this is new as a science remains to be seen. But we may fully appreciate the new attentiveness to awe that invites us to wonder and not to either explanation or exploitation. Such a posture compels the practitioners of awe to recognize that there is something greater, more hidden, and more sublime than our explanatory practices in science. Of course the reality of awe is not new in religious awareness, even if it strikes one as new in a "scientific" perspective. The rendering of awe in biblical poetry is through the singing of doxology in the recognition that the base, bottom, and ground of what we are is rooted in a reality other than us. Thus pietists have for a very long time engaged with and practiced the doxological awe voiced in the Bible. Such doxologies refer to the one who stands outside of all of our explanatory categories and beyond our naming.

- The book of Psalms breaks open all explanatory categories, and invites to doxologies of wonder:

*By awesome deeds [*nora'oth*] you answer us with deliverance,*
O God of our salvation;
you are the hope of all the ends of the earth
and of the farthest seas.
By your strength you established the mountains;
you are girded with might.
You silence the roaring of the seas,
the roaring of their waves,
the tumult of the peoples.
Those who live at earth's farthest bounds are awed [yiyra'] by your signs;
you make the gateways of the morning and the evening shout for joy. (Ps 65:5–8)

He sends out his command to the earth;
his word runs swiftly.
He gives snow like wool;
he scatters frost like ashes.
He hurls down hail like crumbs—
who can stand before his cold?
He sends out his word, and melts them;
he makes his wind blow, and the waters flow.
He declares his word to Jacob,
his statutes and ordinances to Israel. (Ps 147:15–19)

Praise the LORD *from the earth,*
you sea monsters and all deeps,

fire and hail, snow and frost,
stormy wind fulfilling his command!
Mountains and all hills,
fruit trees and all cedars!
Wild animals and all cattle,
creeping things and flying birds! (Ps 148:7–10)

The doxological tradition is utilized in the poem of Job as a way of letting the hidden mystery of God escape the explanatory power of Job and his friends:

Where were you when I laid the foundation of the earth?
Tell me, if you have understanding.
Who determined its measurements—surely you know!
Or who stretched the line upon it?
On what were its bases sunk,
or who laid its cornerstone
when the morning stars sang together
and all the heavenly beings shouted for joy?
Or who shut in the sea with doors
when it burst out from the womb?—
when I made the clouds its garment,
and thick darkness its swaddling band,
and prescribed bounds for it,
and set bars and doors,
and said, "Thus far shall you come, and no farther,
and here shall your proud waves be stopped"? (Job 38:4–11)

Do you give the horse its might?
Do you clothe its neck with mane?
Do you make it leap like the locust?
Its majestic snorting is terrible.

It paws violently, exults mightily;
it goes out to meet the weapons.
It laughs at fear, and is not dismayed;
it does not turn back from the sword.
Upon it rattle the quiver,
the flashing spear, and the javelin.
With fierceness and rage it swallows the ground;
it cannot stand still at the sound of the trumpet.
When the trumpet sounds, it says "Aha!"
From a distance it smells the battle,
the thunder of the captains, and the shouting.
(Job 39:19–25)

The wonder of God as creator is enough to render Job to silence. Job can recognize that his explanatory capacity to reduce reality to his categories of reason is futile. The holiness of God will not be hemmed in by human knowledge. The faithful community has long known this, while the scientific community, according to Keltner, is ready for a fresh embrace of this reality.

The doxological cadences of the books of Psalms and Job, moreover, are reiterated in the New Testament epistles of Ephesians and Colossians. These epistles make the claim that the rule of Christ extends to all of creation, a claim the pietists gladly echo:

He is the image of the invisible God, the first born of all creation; for in him all things in heaven and on earth were created, things visible and invisible, whether thrones or dominions or rulers or powers—all things have been created through him and for him. He himself is before all things, and in him all things hold together. . . . For in him all the fullness of God was pleased to dwell, and through him God was pleased to reconcile to himself all things, whether on earth or

> *in heaven, by making peace through the blood of his cross.*
> *(Col 1:15–20)*

It is for this reason that these epistles essentially dissolve into doxological wonder. And so it is that pietists refuse the explanatory reductions of *scientism*, but welcome the probes to understanding in responsible *science*. As faith is always playing catch-up to every new emergent in science, so it is not too much to say that science is playing catch-up in its emergent wonder and awe as it embraces appropriate ways to be in awe before the wonder of the creator. In the great pietistic hymn of Charles Wesley, we are at the end not fixed in explanation. We are, rather, "lost in wonder, love, and praise." It is for that reason that pietism is a singing tradition. The deep claims of faith cannot be rendered in explanatory rationality, even though the theological tradition continues to try to do that. They can only be voiced in the cadences of trust and wonder that allow for the closest intimacy with holiness, while at the same time affirming the complete "otherness" of that holiness.

Pietism is not put off by science. It insists, however, that the service rendered by science must be governed by a single criterion, namely, the good or ill that will be done to "the least" (see Matt 25:40, 45). It is always "the least" who turn out to be the ultimate host for God's holiness. Any pretense otherwise—to find God's holiness in doctrine, liturgy, or ethics—is to misconstrue. Pietism anticipates that in the fullness of God's rule, that the *last* will be *first,* thus a reiteration of the way in which the crucified one is seen to be raised to governance. Such a reversal from Good Friday to Easter defies all of our most cunning knowledge.

It turns out that the generative tension between scientific knowledge and trusting faith is well voiced by the ancient sage in Israel:

> *It is the glory of God to* conceal *things,*
> *but the glory of kings to* search things out. *(Prov 25:2)*

It is human work to search things out, the work of science. It is the work of the holy God to conceal from such study the mystery of life. That context between *searching out* and *concealing* goes on and on. Human freedom in such work is definitional. It does so, however, amid the awesome rule of God. This much the pietists understood intuitively. That is why we *bow in worship* before the holy God, while *welcoming* the best work of science.

10

THE GOD OF THE OTHER

AFTER THE MEMORY of Moses, the daring of David, and the opulence of Solomon, ancient Israel came to believe that it was God's chosen people who had a monopoly on God's love and God's goodness.* In the eighth century BCE the prophet Amos took as his work to help his contemporaries in Israel to see that Israel in its chosenness had no monopoly on God's goodness. Its chosenness was no pass from obedience to God's rule, and no guarantee of God's love.

Thus in his Oracles against the Nations Amos shows, one by one, that Israel's neighbors and adversaries were subject to God's rule and God judgment (Amos 1–2). Surprisingly, he also includes Judah (2:4–5) and Israel (2:6–11) among those called to harsh account by God. And then, in one of his most remarkable utterances, Amos says this:

> *Are you not like the Ethiopians to me,*
> *O people of Israel? says the LORD.*
> *Did I not bring Israel from the land of Egypt,*
> *and the Philistines from Caphtor and the Arameans from Kir? (Amos 9:7)*

Israel remembered its emancipation from slavery in Egypt under Pharaoh, and imagined that God's exodus deliverance was a singular act without parallel in the history of the world. After all, God had identified Israel as "my first born son" (Exod 4:22). But Amos, to the contrary, insisted otherwise. He asks of Israel two rhetorical questions.

---

* First published in *America Magazine*.

The first question requires a yes from Israel. Yes, Israel is like the Ethiopians. That must have been a surprise and a shock to Israel, to hear itself compared to Ethiopia, a nation of "colored people." Amos challenges the exclusionary self-understanding of Israel. In his second rhetorical question Amos probes the meaning of the exodus deliverance with the verb "bring up from," that is, "set free from." Yes, God did bring up Israel from Egypt; without a doubt! Everyone knows that. But then two other claims:

> *Yes, YHWH did* bring up *the Philistines from Caphtor.*
> *Yes, YHWH did bring up the Arameans (Syrians) from Kir.*

Amos names two foreign peoples that were at different times Israel's most threatening enemies, the Philistines and later the Syrians. He dares to say that God enacts "exoduses" for Israel's enemies. He affirms that God' emancipatory power extends to other peoples who are not commonly taken to be "chosen." He debunks Israel's claim to the exclusionary love and justice of God, and insists that in universal scope YHWH's emancipatory reach extends everywhere, at many times, and in many places, bringing emancipation for those not yet liberated. Indeed, he suggests that the wide sweep of history under YHWH is a sequence of exoduses, so that there is nothing exclusionary about Israel's emancipatory memory or claim.

Thus we may consider an inventory of *the chosen* and *the unchosen* whom God emancipates:

a) *Israel* has no doubt it was "the chosen people" and now Amos says, to the contrary, even Israel's enemies are subject to YHWH's emancipatory intention.
b) *White people*, in our modern world, take themselves to be God's chosen people. Thus white European culture is the most "advanced" with its colonial exploitation and its mastery in

arts, science, and wealth. And now Amos, to the contrary, dares to say that "people of color" (represented by the Ethiopians) are also subject to God's emancipatory love. God's love is not exclusively for white people, even though Europeans who came to America took their whiteness as a privileged status, and had few qualms about imitating Pharaoh in enslaving people of color.

c) For much too long a time it has been easy to see that *males* are God's chosen people. They are the ones with power who have been able to shape history and accumulate wealth. They are the ones for whom the verbs "exploit conquer, occupy, possess" most readily apply. And then the prophetic tradition, extended and enacted through the testimony and ministry of Jesus, showed that God's emancipatory love reached effectively toward females. Thus Mary Magdalene was among the earliest disciples of Jesus. And Paul can declare that in Christ there is neither "male nor female." The gender revolution continues as women are increasingly welcomed into the public life of the world, and even, belatedly, into the ministry of the church.

d) Anyone can see that *straight persons* are the chosen of God who have been able to define social power and social acceptability. Anyone who "deviated" from the straight world has been excluded forever from social acceptance, has been deemed a danger and a threat to social well-being, and thus subject to harsh treatment. And now, belatedly, we are able to see that the reach of God's emancipatory love extends beyond readily approved straight people to include LGBTQ persons, who have been much too long held in the bondage of social censorship and social disapproval. The passion of God's emancipatory embrace goes well beyond straight people!

We can see, historically, that these several emancipatory concerns have come to fruition very slowly and to some extent in sequence:

First, *Gentiles* beyond chosen Israel;
Then, *people of color* beyond whites;
Later, *females* beyond males, and
Very belatedly *LGBTQ persons* beyond straight hegemony.

But it has happened and continues to happen in all of these traditions! God's truth is marching on! We are discerning that God's love, justice, freedom, mercy, and faithfulness cannot be contained in our self-imagined categories of chosenness and privilege. Our several orthodoxies of nationalism, racism, sexism, and gender exclusion all have imagined a God who could be safely kept in our preferred boundaries. But *the God of the covenant* who is *the God the Gospel* will not be so contained. Indeed, it is evident that God's peculiar attentiveness is especially drawn toward those who are regularly denied legitimacy in our social arrangements. We can knowingly speak of "God's preferential option" not only for the poor but toward all those who are otherwise discounted.

It seems clear enough that all such efforts to box in the God of freedom are grounded in fear. We imagine that the other—the ones unlike us—are a threat, and so we fashion exclusionary practices and rules. It turns out, however, that such fear is not the last word. God intends us, all those who are chosen—whites, males, straight—to see that faith, hope and love are stronger than fear and will prevail.

And so the other need not be a threat, but can be welcomed as a neighbor

Because the reach of emancipation toward LGBTQ persons is the latest such move toward liberation, we may pay special attention to the way in which it sounds through the lines of Amos:

Are you not like the LBGTQ persons to me, O straights? Yes!
Did I not bring up straight people to be emancipated agents in
the world? Yes!

And did I not bring up LGBTQ persons to first-class citizenship in the world? Yes!
And did I not bring up LGBTQ persons to be free for a life of joy and freedom and well-being in the world? Yes!

Like the earlier questions posed by Amos, these world-shattering questions of Amos require a vigorous yes in response. It is a yes of gospel emancipation. It is a yes of limitless love. It is a yes of well-being that counters all of our fearful exclusions. Amos could not have been popular among the "chosen" for such utterance. That, however, is not much against his bold truth-telling. The good news summons us to a vigorous, unafraid yes toward all those whom the Pharaohs of the world continue to keep in bondage. As the apostle Paul concludes,

For freedom Christ has set us free. Stand firm, therefore, and do not submit again to a yoke of slavery. (Gal 5:1)

11

THE EMPOWERING, ILLUMINATING WORD FROM ELSEWHERE

Your word is a lamp to my feet
and a light to my path.

Psalm 119:105

A FEW SUNDAYS ago, our well-spoken pastor, Joan, recited this biblical verse as the salutation at the outset of her sermon. She did not comment further on the verse but proceeded in a compelling way to articulate the "path/way" of the gospel to which the verse refers.

I have long had a special personal attachment to this verse. In my growing up context of evangelical pietism in the "E and R" tradition, it was the custom that the pastor assigned to each thirteen-year-old confirmand a "confirmation verse." That verse was taken to be a marker of faith for the confirmand and was often recalled and reiterated many years later at the funeral of the deceased confirmand. In my case, my pastor (also my father) assigned this as my confirmation verse. Nothing was made of it at the time, but for a long time now in retrospect I have pondered my father's choice of the verse for me, given that I have spent my adult life engaged with and expositing the "word" of the biblical text. As a consequence, I have taken his assignment of this verse to me as a thirteen-year-old as a providential act in anticipation of the adult life and work that have long occupied me.

The verse occurs in the longest of the Psalms, Psalm 119. That long psalm is shaped as the most artful and well-developed acrostic poem in scripture. An "acrostic" is a poetic articulation that proceeds through the alphabet with each successive line beginning with the next letter from *A* to *Z*, that is in Hebrew, from *'aleph* to *taw*. We have other acrostic poems in the Old Testament that run the course of the alphabet as a way of completeness. (See Ps 25, 34, 37, 111, 145, and Prov 31:10–31, Lam 1–4.) The scholar who has most intently and vigorously studied the acrostic pattern is J. P. Fokkelman (*Major Poems of the Hebrew Bible: At the Interface of Prosody and Structural Analysis* [Leiden, 2000]). In each of these texts the alphabetic sequence is traced, though some of the poetry does not complete the task. Psalm 119, however, is exceptional. In all the other cases of acrostic each letter of the Hebrew alphabet occurs once in sequence. In Psalm 119, by contrast, each letter gets eight successive lines. Thus with twenty-two letters in the alphabet, and each letter reiterated eight times, we get a sum of 176 verses. It is for that reason that the psalm is so long. Our verse 105 occurs as the first of eight verses that start with *nun* (*n*) (vv. 105–12). The first word in verse 105, the first of eight lines with *nun*, is *ner* ("lamp"). Unfortunately none of this is evident in English translation.

One can readily see in the psalm a cluster of terms that are variously repeated and reiterated:

> *Commandment, decree, judgment, law (Torah), ordinance, precept, statute, word.*

We may take all of these several terms as rough synonyms, all of which refer to the written Torah. The written Torah (never without thick interpretation) is a "lamp" and a "light." It serves to illumine the path/way in which covenanted Israel is to walk. We may notice the same parallelism in Jeremiah 6:16:

> *Thus says the* L*ORD:*
> *Stand at the crossroads, and look,*
>   *and ask for the ancient paths,*

where the good way lies; and walk in it,
and find rest for your souls.

The ancient path/way is surely the way of Torah that Jeremiah commended in chapter 11. In this verse the prophet laments that Israel has chosen not to walk in that path/way. Concerning the parallelism, remarkably in Proverbs 8:20, personified wisdom affirms the substance of the way/path commended in covenant:

I (wisdom) walk in the way of righteousness,
and the paths of justice.

The path/way of Torah is the righteousness and justice that enact love of God and love of neighbor. While wisdom commends that way/path, the prophet sees that Israel refuses to walk in it. Thus in considering the path/way of covenanted Israel, we are able to see the deep insistence and radicality of our verse that is so innocent-looking. The path/way of Israel, enunciated in the Torah of Sinai, is an alternative path/way, alternative to the predation of Pharaoh, alternative to the extravagance of Solomon, and alternative to the brutality of Babylon. It is plausible, moreover, that this cluster of terms in the Psalm refers more explicitly to the book of Deuteronomy and to the trajectory of Torah interpretation that ensues from and is advocated by it. Thus Gerhard von Rad (*Studies in Deuteronomy*, 16 [SCM, 1953]), could see that Deuteronomy was "preached law," so that the preaching (interpretive proclamation) of the Torah of Deuteronomy became the engine of Judaism as reflected in the leadership of Ezra and in the sermonic content of the Books of Chronicles, on which see Gerhard von Rad, "The Levitical Sermon in I and 2 Chronicles," in *The Problem of the Hexateuch and Other Essays*, 1966 (267–80), and Jacob M. Myers, "The Kerygma of the Chronicler," *Interpretation* XX (1966): 259.

This same trajectory of an alternative path/way comes to clear expression in the teaching of Jesus:

> *Enter through the narrow gate; for the gate is wide and the road is easy that leads to destruction, and there are many who take it. For the gate is narrow and the road is hard that leads to life, and there are few who find it. (Matt 7:13–14; see Luke 13:24)*

In the horizon of Jesus, this path/way consisted in discipleship that required leaving all else to "follow." This characterization of the alternative community around Jesus as "followers of the way" (Acts 9; 24:14) indicates the requirements that we know as "love of God" and "love of neighbor." This narrow, hard way is an alternative to the broad, easy way of the world marked by self-sufficiency and self-securing. Discipleship to Jesus is indeed an articulation of covenantal obedience to the alternative of Torah. The Torah provides guidance and illumination for how to live this alternative life in the world.

Alternatively, Karl Barth parses the matter differently. He takes "the word" to be the decisive articulation of God. It is this logos (logic that pervades creation) that is the force of the creator who "calls the world into being." It is, moreover, this same word that is bodily present in the person of Jesus "full of grace and truth." But then boldly, Barth goes further to aver that the word that creates and the word that is enfleshed in Jesus is the word as the written witness of Scripture that comes to powerful performance in the word as sermon. This breath-taking force of the word in these several modes is contrasted to a world "formless and void" that is without the ordering, life-giving power of the word. Such a world devoid of the word is a world unto death.

All of this was readily on the table when our pastor moved easily from the initial salutation to her sermon on John 6:3–13 and the wonder of the loaves multiplied in order to feed a hungry crowd. She nicely finessed every "explanation" for the delivery of bread, as the four Gospels, each in turn, refuses to "explain" this spectacular wonder. The text is a story, not an argument. It is a specific narrative, not a logical syllogism. The wonder of the narrative is the affirmation that in the fleshly word of Jesus's own person the capacity of the creator God for abundance is readily available. Our pastor traced through two other narratives of abundant bread: the manna story of Exodus 16, and the wonder of bread wrought through Elisha (2 Kings 4:42–44). Her proclamation concerned the radical claim that the world governed by the creator God teems with life-giving abundance, an abundance that is quite unlike and contrasted with the world around us that is dominated by fear, greed, and violence, and thus by scarcity.

The sermon concerned the demanding either/or of scarcity/abundance. There is no doubt that our present world is powerfully dominated by an ideology of scarcity. It is this ideology that propels tax policy, readiness for war, and our greedy arguments for the exclusion and disregard of the poor, the vulnerable, and the "undeserving." The claim of the sermon—the claim of the Torah, the claim of the gospel—is that we may walk in the light that illumines a different path of glad obedience in the world. (On the parallel claims in Judaism and Christianity, see James A. Sanders, "Torah and Christ," *Interpretation* 29 [1975].) In ancient Israel that walk is the way/path of covenant. In the story of Jesus, it is the glad walk of discipleship. Taken either way, it is a summons to live differently, to live with the truth of God's abundance in a way that resists and refuses the fear of scarcity so evident in our society. It follows that on that path/way we may be free of fear and of greed and (consequently) free of every temptation to violence.

I had two thoughts as I reflected on my confirmation verse and the sermon that followed it a few Sundays ago. First, I understood afresh the South African hymn, "Siyahamba":

We are marching in the light,
We are marching in the light of God,
We are marching in the light of God,
We are marching, marching,
We are marching. . . .

That "march" about which Blacks sing in South Africa is a march of faith that resists, rejects, and refuses the social reality of apartheid and exclusiveness. That has been a hard, risky march in South Africa, just as it is always a hard, demanding alternative to the easier path of the status quo.

Second, as we gathered to hear our pastor line out the alternative path/way of abundance and generosity, it dawned on me afresh that serious discipleship requires that we be at the meeting of the faithful regularly, always again, in order to participate in the performance of the alternative path/way. The reason we must always be at the meeting of the faithful is that we are regularly and forcefully bombarded by the regnant path/way of scarcity. Indeed, our pastor began her sermon by pointing out how the narrative of scarcity was everywhere pervasive including in the interminable TV ads. It is the work of "the meeting" to counter that bombardment, and to remind us of our alternative path/way. The utterance of the word does indeed guide our path/way. Without that word uttered and heard we may, much too readily, stray to the wide, easy path of scarcity that leads to "destruction" (Matt 7:13)!

Part IV

NEW ECONOMY

I think three things about the need for the church. First of all, the church, with all its flaws, keeps the story alive. Fundamentalist churches, for which I have no truck, keep the story alive, which is urgent. The second thing is that in any community where there's any trouble, you will find the church there. I often entertain the thought, What would this community be like if it took the churches out of it? It would be a less humane place. And the third thing is that that all of my best friends are church people. It's a place to be with people who share something of the vision and have the resolve that I care about. Recently I went to a neighborhood dinner to welcome one of our new pastors and there were probably twenty people there, some of them I didn't know. But there was a couple there who every year do a garden that produces food for the poor of our county. There was a couple who are caring for a disabled child and bringing her to a good life. There was another couple there who was doing something else extraordinary. These were very ordinary people who are doing extraordinary things rather innocently, without calling attention to themselves. And that seems to me the church at its best. They had no great interest in theology. They probably couldn't have said why they were doing it, they just went about it. And I love being with people like that.

12

LET'S DO THE NUMBERS

AS OFTEN AS I can, I listen to Kai Ryssdal in his NPR program, *Marketplace*. As every listener knows, Ryssdal has a feature every night in which he says, "Let's do the numbers." This is the moment when he reviews the market gains and losses for the day. Thus I borrow my title from his show. I have been thinking about numbers as a way of telling the story of our common life. That inescapably has led me to consider "living by the numbers" or "telling by numbers" in the Bible.

It has occurred to me that in the Bible the character who most prominently (and most successfully?) lived by numbers is King Solomon. So here are Solomon's numbers as reported in his narrative, running from the smallest to the larger, to the largest numbers. I am not sure I got them all, but here are enough to see what it was like for Israel's great king to be remembered via numbers as one who lived by and for the numbers:

120 talents of gold (1 Kings 10:10);
200 large shields (10:16);
300 concubines (11:3);
420 talents of gold (9:28);
550 work supervisors (9:23);
600 shekels of gold (10:16);
600 talents of silver as the cost of a chariot (10:29);
666 talents of gold (10:14);
700 princesses (11:3);
1005 songs (4:32);
1400 chariots (10:26);

3000 proverbs (4:32);
3300 work supervisors (5:16);
12,000 horses (10:26);
22,000 oxen sacrificed (8:63);
30,000 forced laborers in Israel (5:13);
70,000 laborers (5:15);
80,000 stonecutters (5:15); and
120,000 sheep sacrificed (8:63).

It is easy enough to see that Solomon lived *by the numbers* and *for the numbers*. For good reason he had in his inchoate bureaucracy *secretaries* (Elihoreph and Ahijah) (*sopherim*) and a *recorder* (Jehoshaphat) (*mazkir*) (1 Kings 4:3). One could imagine that "cabinet meetings" were largely decisions about numbers concerning income and expenditure, and the implications of these numbers for grand royal plans.

We can identify accent points among these numbers:

1. It was all about *money*! His regime was funded by a predatory tax system (see 4:7–19, 12:1–19), and by aggressive trade as an arms dealer. Everything was an exhibit of wealth accumulated by the king.
2. It was all about *security*! Thus we imagine that Solomon's regime is a forceful forerunner of "the security state" of our own time in which vast resources were invested in security, here in the form of chariots and horses.
3. It was all about the maintenance and control of a huge *work force* that worked in constructing fortresses and grandiose royal buildings (1 Kings 7:1–21). The endless building projects required a great work force, much of it consisting in the enslavement of Solomon's own Israelite people (1 Kings 5:13). This in turn required a large company of work supervisors, so that one can conclude that his aggressive labor policies fittingly reprised those of Pharaoh, his father-in-law (see Exod 5).

4. We may well imagine that Solomon's exhibit of wealth and his limitless compulsion for acquisition culminated in his collection of women as *wives and concubines*. Thus his extended harem was an extended exhibit of his wealth and no doubt of his virility as well. The collection of women often turns out to be the ultimate exhibit of power for men who endlessly accumulate and acquire, often *ad seriatim*.
5. Given Solomon's urge to self-exhibit, it is not surprising that even his worship of the state God, YHWH, (who was rooted in old tribal traditions that were alien to Solomon) should evoke more of his grandiose energy. Thus in addition to the exhibitionist propensity of his temple, his over-the-top sacrifice of sheep and oxen at the dedication of his temple must have been a powerful (even if bloody!) reminder that his extravagance knew no limit: 22,000 oxen and 120,000 sheep in a day (1 Kings 8:63)! We may judge that he would have had no comprehension of the prophetic assertion of Micah 6:8 concerning justice, kindness, and humility; but he would have reveled in the extravagance of Micah 6:7 concerning "thousands of rams" and "ten thousand rivers of oil." He likely would not have noticed that the prophetic lines are ironic.
6. Given the endless exhibit of his success, it does not surprise that the king is a prominent "*patron of the arts*" in his sponsorship of proverbs and songs, perhaps with the maintenance of a guild of "the wise" (his own house intellectuals), along with temple choirs (see 1 Chronicles 25:1–31). When we consider all six facets of this royal exhibit, we can see that Solomon's public piety clearly was part of his passion for big numbers. We can conclude, further, that living by the numbers means an incessant quest for "more," and thus growth, expansion, and predation in every dimension of society were the order of the day. It seems plausible, if not likely, that definition by numbers (big numbers!) must have sapped whatever "human" energy for justice

> and righteousness that may have been present in the regime. The numbers function for Solomon to ensure his accumulation, acquisition, and predation, a show of his self-sufficient power.

Surely there is some fine irony in the fact that of only two psalms dedicated to Solomon (the other one is Ps 127, which speaks of a generative man) is Psalm 72, which speaks as a charter for a just king by whose practice of justice for the poor and needy will sustain a successful domain:

> *Give the king your justice, O God,*
> *and your righteousness to a king's son.*
> *May he judge your people with righteousness,*
> *and your poor with justice.*
> *May the mountains yield prosperity for the people,*
> *and the hills, in righteousness.*
> *May he defend the cause of the poor of the people,*
> *give deliverance to the needy,*
> *and crush the oppressor. . . .*
> *May he have dominion from sea to sea,*
> *and from the River to the ends of the earth.*
> *May his foes bow down before him,*
> *and his enemies lick the dust.*
> *May the kings of Tarshish and of the isles*
> *render him tribute,*
> *may the kings of Sheba and Seba*
> *bring gifts.*
> *May all kings fall down before him,*
> *all nations give him service. (Ps 72:1–4, 8–11)*

The narrative of Solomon fully and dramatically contradicts the hopes and promises of the psalm, suggesting the high social cost of living by the numbers.

With a Solomonic accent on big numbers, I looked to see about big numbers in the New Testament. As far as I know, we get only two big numbers for Jesus, both concerning his miracles of food:

> *Those who had eaten the loaves numbered* five thousand *men. (Mark 6:44)*
>
> *Now there were about* four thousand *people. (Mark 8:9)*

It is no wonder that he is perplexed that his disciples did not yet understand about the bread:

> *They said to one another, "It is because we have no bread." And becoming aware of it, Jesus said to them, "Why are you talking about having no bread? Do you still not perceive or understand? Are your hearts hardened? Do you have eyes, and fail to see? Do you have ears, and fail to hear? And do you not remember? When I broke the five loaves for the* five thousand, *how many baskets full of broken pieces did you collect?" They said to him, "Twelve." "And the seven for the* four thousand, *how many baskets full of broken pieces did you collect?" And they said to him, "Seven." Then he said to them, "Do you not yet understand?" (Mark 8:16–21)*

Likewise in the Book of Acts there are two big numbers:

> *So those who welcomed his message were baptized, and that day about* three thousand *persons were added. (Acts 2:41)*
>
> *But many of those who heard the word believed; and they numbered about* five thousand. *(Acts 4:4)*

These numbers might have caused Solomon to be envious. A closer look suggests that these numbers in the Gospel narrative and in the Book of Acts serve a purpose very different from the numbers of Solomon.

Whereas the big numbers for Solomon are self-promotional, the big numbers in the New Testament point away from the agents of them (Jesus, Peter and the other apostles, and then Peter and John) in order to exhibit the generous governance of God. In both of these latter cases the numbers, moreover, attest to the reach of God's gift, both of bread and of new life outside the reach of the Roman Empire. Thus in both cases the numbers are transformative, restorative, and emancipatory, a wholesale contrast to the numbers of Solomon that brought with them nothing of transformation, restoration, or emancipation.

My impetus for looking into these numbers at all was an engagement with Steven Conn, *Nothing Succeeds Like Failure: The Sad History of American Business Schools* (Cornell, 2019), and his scathing review of the Harvard Business School and, by implication, business schools in general. Conn opines that the business schools in fact have no substantive curriculum, and no body of literature or research that matters to the programs. Indeed, he judges that the purpose of the business school, with much camouflage, is to make money, and to educate students in the arts of acquisitiveness, even when those arts extend to predatory practices. Thus Conn concludes:

> *For the most part, the institutionalists had made no attempt to hide their political agendas. The neoclassicists who followed them, on the other hand, pretended that they had no policies at all. After all, complex equations have no ideology. By extension, the public policies that flowed from their work, a flow that began in earnest in the 1970s, were packaged as similarly free of ideology. That of course, was and remains utter nonsense. One newspaper had smirked as far back as 1889 that "this science of political economy . . . is subject to change at the polls on election day by the will of the people," and that was no less true in 1989. Yet few of these economists acknowledged that scientific "objectivity" might be less straightforward and more problematic than they insisted it*

> *was—even as physicists and other scientists were becoming more aware of the contingent nature of their own work. What the neoclassicists sold, then, amounted to morality tales masquerading as mathematics. (110)*

While appeal to "differential equations and lots of graphs" yielded the impression of objectivity and intellectual innocence, in fact the ideological tilt of such programs are easy enough to detect, namely, the making of money. Thus Conn sees that the great preoccupation with numbers is not just mathematics, but "morality tales." It is the morality of a neoliberal persuasion that justifies making money at the expense of public well-being.

Conn goes on to mock the pretense of business schools with their scarcely concealed agenda by quoting Philip Delves Broughton:

> *I write as the carrier of an MBA from the Harvard Business School—once regarded as a ticket to riches, but these days more like the scarlet letters of shame. . . . We MBAs are haunted by the thought that the tag really stands for Mediocre But Arrogant, Mighty Big Attitude, Me Before Anyone and Management by Accident. For today's purposes, perhaps it should be Monsters of the Business Apocalypse. (155)*

As I write in chapter 14, the Columbia University Business School, with its new grand building, is seeking a focal point beyond making money in order to render more public good. Clearly in the sober judgment of Conn, the business schools have not yet seriously departed from an ideology that justifies the accumulation of generous private wealth. It is not difficult to see that the big numbers in the differential equations and graphs serve a purpose not unlike the big numbers of Solomon that served only his predatory appetite.

We are not surprised to observe that Jesus is the very antithesis of the big numbers of Solomon. Thus in his Sermon on the Mount,

Jesus ponders the anxiety of his disciples and the provisions made by the creator that will sustain creaturely life:

> *Can any of you by worrying add a single hour to your span of life? And why do you worry about clothing? Consider the lilies of the field, how they grow; they neither toil nor spin, yet I tell you,* even Solomon *in all his glory was not clothed like one of these. (Matt 6:27–29)*

It turns out that except for the two "wonders" of his "wonder bread," Jesus was quite content with small numbers:

- two sons (Luke 15:11);
- ten lepers (Luke 17:12);
- twelve disciples (Mark 10:41; ten plus two!).

And so the same when the early church could settle for only seven deacons (Acts 6:3).

It is not a surprise that the church, after the manner of Jesus, is committed to the work of transformation, restoration, and emancipation. It is not a surprise that this work cannot be done "wholesale." The work requires patience, attentiveness, and long-term engagement with those with whom we minister. To be sure, the church is sometimes bewitched by the big numbers of the world, and yearns for more members, more dollars, and more programs. The church sometimes yearns to be "successful" when measured by the numerical fascinations of our society. But we know better! We know better because the Lord of the church has shown us and taught us differently. He exhibited a patient strategy of investing with those disregarded in our numerical world. In this time of the church's diminished social importance, we may pause to recognize that the church's measure of faithfulness and effectiveness is very different from that of Solomon or of the Harvard Business School. When seventy disciples returned to Jesus with exuberant excitement over their good work of healing the sick and casting out demons, even they do not cite numbers in their report to Jesus (Luke 10:17). Even so, in his response to their exuberance, Jesus cautions his disciples about being overly impressed with the force of their good work. Rather, he invites them to notice "that your names are written in heaven." That is enough—that they were useful vehicles for the transformative, restorative, emancipatory work of the Spirit. He does not ask them for numbers, but takes notice of their faithfulness.

The contrast of Jesus to the number crunchers, ancient and contemporary, readily calls to mind the Talmudic saying in which Jesus is rooted:

Save one life and you save the world.

That ancient saying was notably revivified by Oscar Schindler in his rescue work of jeopardized Jews. In fact the saying is often reperformed by those who are not bewitched by numbers, but who yield to the summons to do proper human work. Next time you hear Kai Ryssdal on *Marketplace*, remember that there are extensive spheres of our common life that are not measured by "the numbers." We might judge that the great either/or in this matter is clear and stark:

accumulation, acquisition, predation
or
transformation, restoration, emancipation.

13

MONEY TALK IN THE CHURCH

SOMEWHAT HAPHAZARDLY THE church has always had to talk about money. It has talked about money because of its ongoing concern for "stewardship" and the church budget. Now however, it is clear that the church's talk about money cannot be confined to its own finances, but must concern the economy with its endless propensity for injustice and inequality, for example, regressive taxation, high interest rates, and low wages. The reason the church has to talk about the economy is because there is almost no one left to think and talk critically about the economy because of the dominance of capitalist ideology and its capacity to domesticate almost every voice. What follows here is a consideration of some of the biblical texts to which we may appeal in our "money talk," while we recognize that all such talk in the church is hazardous and risky. Most specifically, we need to talk about the toxic power of debt, and to do so in many congregations that are occupied by vigilant creditors who benefit from the perennially indebted.

It occurs to me that we may find in the Bible two quite different ways of talking about money concerning which we need to have clarity. One way to talk about money in the Bible is to think of economic transactions in *an individualistic way*, as simple exchanges that take place between two parties or persons, often a creditor and a debtor. This view, featured especially in the book of Proverbs, understands the use of money in the following way with an accent on individual responsibility and freedom:

- Having money requires hard work:

A slack hand causes poverty,
but the hand of the diligent makes rich. (Prov 10:4)

A little sleep, a little slumber,
a little folding of the hands to rest,
and poverty will come upon you like a robber,
and want, like an armed warrior. (24:33–34)

- Greed that oppresses the vulnerable is destructive:

Oppressing the poor in order to enrich oneself,
and giving to the rich, will lead only to loss. (22:16)

Do not rob the poor because they are poor,
or crush the afflicted at the gate;
for the Lord *pleads their cause*
and despoils of life those who despoil them. (22:22–23)

- Debt must be avoided:

It is senseless to give a pledge,
to become surety for a neighbor. (17:18)

The rich rules over the poor,
and the borrower is the slave of the lender. (22:7)

- Generosity toward the needy is commended:

Those who despise their neighbors are sinners,
but happy are those who are kind to the poor. (14:21)

Whoever gives to the poor will lack nothing,
but one who turns a blind eye will get many a curse. (28:27)

All of these maxims assume that economics is the simple practice of unencumbered individuals who may take responsibility for their future. The downside of this teaching is the assumption that failure in the economy is a sign of individual failure, perhaps laziness or foolishness or carelessness.

This way of talking about money is widely held by unthinking church members and by the wider US public. This view was given clear, harsh expression by Ralph Waldo Emerson in his famous essay, *Self-Reliance:*

> *Debt, grinding debt, whose iron face the widow, the orphan and the sons of genius fear and hate . . . is a preceptor whose lessons cannot be foregone, and is needed most by those who suffer from it most.*
>
> *[Emerson judged that] the cessation of profit, rent, and interest would make all men idle and immoral. [Most of the poor] have made themselves so, [and under socialism would] prove a burden on the state.*

Such a self-congratulatory tone reflects a naiveté that makes critical reflection on money exceedingly difficult.

An alternative view of money *in systemic terms* is much more fully explored in Scripture. In this view, there is recognition of the complexity of the economy and the way in which the power of money operates well beyond the simplicity of individual claims and practices. We may take the narrative of Genesis 47:13–26 as a forceful articulation of a sophisticated understanding of money. (It is a text that is never read aloud in church.) In the narrative, Joseph, beloved son of Jacob, has become the money man for Pharaoh, who is himself an embodiment and symbol of coercive economic dominance in his realm. In this narrative Pharaoh has a monopoly on grain, as he has stored his surplus grain in the storage cities built by Israelite slave labor (Exod 1:11). There is, to be sure, some high irony in the recognition that the storehouse cities that gave Pharaoh a monopoly were built by slave labor. (See James C. Scott, *Against the Grain: A Deep History of the Earliest States* [Yale, 2017], as he explores the way in which grain was the most likely instrument in the ancient world for accumulation of wealth and power.) Amid the food shortage of the famine, Joseph, on behalf of Pharaoh, traded royal grain for the money of the subsistence peasants (v. 14). When the money of the peasants was gone, Joseph, on behalf of Pharaoh, traded royal grain for the livestock of the peasants, their means of production (vv. 16–17). When their money and their livestock (means of production) had been seized and the famine continued, Joseph, on behalf of Pharaoh, traded royal grain for their land and their bodies, and made them willing slaves of the state economy (vv. 19, 25). In the end, Pharaoh, through Joseph's mechanisms, had occupied the land and created a system of debt slavery of those so vulnerable that they could not resist the force of Pharaoh's economic power. The narrative is one of the slow, deliberate process of the reduction of the economically vulnerable to a state of *dependency* and, therefore, economic *slavery*. This systemic view of the economy makes clear how innocent (and irrelevant) the simplistic teaching on money in the Book of Proverbs is that fails to reckon with the measure of coercive force that comes with disproportionate wealth.

It is an elemental work of ministry, in my judgment, to help people move from an innocent individualistic account of money to one that reckons with the systemic force of wealth, the core of which is recurringly to reduce the vulnerable to dependence and finally to servile status. Both views of money are to be found in Scripture. That simply means that many different interests had a part in making the tradition. But it is the systemic view of money in Genesis 47 that more fully relates to our current economic reality in which the political force of money generates much of our public life, policy, and practice. Pharaoh fully understood how to exercise that force!

A systemic view of money—variously articulated by the prophets of Israel in their defense of the poor and vulnerable—produced an economy of haves and have-nots, and consigned many subsistence peasants to a life of poverty and vulnerability. The makers of the

Israelite tradition saw this well and clearly. The decisive response to this systemic management of an economy that preyed on the vulnerable is the articulation of the "Year of Release" in *Deuteronomy 15:1–18* and the "Year of Jubilee" in Leviticus 25. The Torah provision for a Year of Release provided that every seven years debts must be canceled and property returned to its rightful owner, in order to prevent the formation of a permanent economic underclass in Israel, for such a class would be profoundly inimical to the notion of a covenantal neighborhood. The Torah teaching on the Year of Release, in the mouth of Moses, features five "absolute infinitives," a grammatical device in Hebrew wherein the verb is reiterated for the purpose of emphasis. The five absolutes infinitives (that are recognized in English translation) are

really hear (v. 7),
really open (v. 8),
willingly lend (v. 8),
give liberally (v. 10), and
really open (V.11).

The five usages (that occur more than anywhere else in Scripture), taken together, underscore the absolute urgency of the practice of debt cancellation. This practice is indeed the antidote to the predatory inclination of the economy. Thus the Torah proposes disrupting conventional economics in the interest of nurturing a neighborhood for the economically encumbered. The juxtaposition of *predation* in Genesis 47 and the *provision for release* in Deuteronomy 15 instruct us in all that we need to know for a critical understanding of our economy. The narrative of predation submerges individual persons into the systemic flow of money; the provision for release, to the contrary, values the vulnerable neighbor enough to resist the force of endless predation.

We may add as suggestive footnotes three textual citations that bespeak a caution to systemic greed:

1. In *1 Samuel 22:2*, David mounts his vigorous campaign against the kingship of Saul. It is reported,

   Everyone who was in distress, and everyone who was in debt, and everyone who was discontented gathered to him; and he became captain over them.

   The triad that characterizes his followers consists of those in distress, in debt, and discontented, those suffering most from present public arrangements. The triad suggests that the company of David consisted in those who are especially vulnerable and therefore prepared for a major social upheaval that David would evoke. The narrative makes no connection to the Year of Release, but we may conclude that David and his company would have had a practical view of redress of economic exploitation, and so supported the new movement. As David Graeber, *Debt: The First 5000 Years* (Melville, 2011), has noted, all such upheavals include, first of all, an effort to burn the tax and bank records that keep vulnerable folk in hock. Such likely are the partisans of David.
2. The Elisha narratives in 2 Kings are deeply subversive of established order. (See Brueggemann, *Testimony to Otherwise* [Chalice, 2001]). In *2 Kings 4:1–7*, we have a narrative concerning a widow woman without resources, who lacked a male advocate in a patriarchal society, and who is at the mercy of predatory creditors (v. 1). In the narrative Elisha responds to the widow's crisis. He enables the widow woman to resist the predation by an act that lacks explanation and defies any normal economic reckoning:

   He said, "Go outside, borrow vessels from all your neighbors, empty vessels and not just a few. Then go in, and shut the door behind you and your children, and start pouring into

all these vessels; when each is full, set it aside." So she left him and shut the door behind her and her children; they kept bringing vessels to her, and she kept pouring. When the vessels were full, she said to her son, "Bring me another vessel." But he said to her, "There are no more." (2 Kings 4:3–6)

The prophet worked an inexplicable abundance for the hapless woman who lacked resources. Her abundance was a prophetic defiance of the economy of parsimony. The narrative concludes as the prophet instructs the widow:

Go sell the oil and pay your debts, and you and your children can live on the rest. (v. 7)

Elisha knew her debts had to be paid. But his provision for her went well beyond her debt. The narrative attests an *inexplicable abundance* wrought by the prophet that makes the *unbearable parsimony* of the credit-debt system to be an irrelevance.

3. *Nehemiah 10:28–39* constitutes a summary of the covenant into which Ezra led Israel in the re-formation of the community of Judaism. The summary offers a number of provisions concerning money and offerings, suggesting that the covenant pertains to the specific monetary practices of the community. Our interest is in the singular notation in 10:31:

We will forego the crops of the seventh year and the exaction of every debt.

Alongside the provision for Sabbath is the mention of a seventh year of debt relief. There is no explanatory account for this provision; but quite clearly this passing note alludes back to the Torah provision of Deuteronomy 15. The notation is an acknowledgment that the economic perspective of the newly formed covenant community was grounded in debt relief that defied "ordinary economics."

Thus we may conclude that while the actual implementation of the Year of Release in ancient Israel is difficult and obscure, there is no doubt that covenantal teaching about the economy refused to accept the ordinary predatory practices of the Pharaonic economy that was replicated among the "Canaanites." This provision is richly evident in the exegetical tradition, as Israel knew that the Lord of the economy does not intend to have the life of the human community reduced to a contest between greedy creditors and helpless debtors. This prospect of relief from the predatory system is elemental to Israel's self-understanding.

It is too far afield from my competence to comment fully on the matter of debt and debt cancellation as the theme operates in the New Testament. But two comments seem especially pertinent.

First, we all know that debt forgiveness is pivotal to the "Lord's Prayer." Thus we pray, "Forgive us our debts as we forgive our debtors" (Matt 6:12). (The alternative conventional reading as "trespasses" does not change anything in the petition.) Sharon Ringe, *Jesus, Liberation, and the Biblical Jubilee* (1985) has shown how this provision and the entire prayer more generally pertain to the Jubilee practice of debt cancellation and restoration to a viable neighborly community. The hard matter of money has been there in our defining prayer from the outset, so we have mumbled and managed to explain away the topic in our long-term effort to keep Jesus safely remote from our economic existence. No doubt the Torah provision of Moses rings in the ears of Jesus!

Second, the parable of the unforgiving servant sounds the same note (Matt 18:23–34). In the parable the king cancels the debt of his desperate servant. That servant in turn, however, refuses to forgive a lesser debt for a fellow slave. The parable jarringly contrasts the *generous forgiveness* of the king and the *pernicious insistence* of the slave.

It is unmistakable that the Torah designation of covenantal economics persists in the narrative reflection of the New Testament. It remains for the church to recover this awareness about the economy in our tradition, and to recover the courage necessary to contest the predatory practices of our economy that have become normative in our society. In sum, Scripture is an attestation to an alternative economy of generosity that is wise and knowing about the system and force of predation. It will not do for church folk to remain "innocent" about this truth telling in Scripture.

If all of that were not enough, we may notice that David Graeber, in his remarkable book, *Debt: The First 5000 Years*, draws the conclusion that the only way out of the morass of debt among us is the practice of Jubilee and debt cancellation. Graeber evinces no interest in matters scriptural or theological, but finally is pressed by economic reality to the most elemental and most insistent teaching of the Torah. Let the church understand! The church has to talk in daring and compelling ways about money!

14

THE UNENDING WORK OF CONTRADICTION

TWICE IN THE Gospel narrative Jesus declares the ultimate either/or of his life and teaching:

> *You cannot serve God and wealth.*

The saying occurs in his Sermon on the Mount (Matt 6:24) and in Luke after the parable of the rich man and his manager (Luke 16:13). This either/or of Jesus is not inflected or qualified. It cuts to the heart of the choice required by the gospel. It is, moreover, an echo of the radical either/or of Moses concerning covenantal fidelity and obedience:

> *See, I set before you today life and prosperity, death and adversity. (Deut 30:15)*

The either/or in both cases constitutes an insistence that the gospel summons pertains to real life in the real world, and not to any privatized otherworldliness.

This declaration of Jesus is the subject of the shrewd discerning discussion of Eugene McCarraher in his book, *The Enchantments of Mammon: How Capitalism Became the Religion of Modernity* (Belknap, 2019). The subtitle indicates his subject, one that is surely obvious and correct, that capitalism is "the religion of modernity" concerning the aggressive state, the ultimacy of the market, and the unfettered predatory freedom of unencumbered individuals. And because the either/or of Jesus has been settled among us as the "or" of mammon, the claim of the "religion of modernity" must receive close and continuing attention from the community clustered around Jesus.

McCarraher traces the way the social gospel of Puritan rootage morphed into predatory capitalism, which has produced what he terms the "fundamental dilemma of the elect" (117). His phrasing is of immense importance:

> *Their quest for a beloved community built on the foundations of capitalist enterprise. (117)*

His phrase "beloved community" refers to the deeply rooted Puritan claim to be "God's chosen people," as subsequent Americans have preferred to treasure the tradition, while committed at the same time to the extremes of capitalism.

Thus at the heart of the modern economic enterprise is the most elemental contradiction, because the "beloved community" with its summons to justice, righteousness, compassion, and generosity cannot and must not be allied with aggressive acquisitiveness. And yet, as can be seen everywhere, our modern economic practice is exactly an embrace of that elemental contradiction.

Indeed, on the day I began working on this chapter (January 7, 2023), the *New York Times* had a telling op-ed piece by James S. Russell, "At Columbia's $600 Million Business School, Time to Rethink Capitalism." The article concerns the new, dazzling architecture of the business school of Columbia University. The subtext for Russell, however, is that the new architecture suggests (requires?) rethinking the long-running commitment of the school to unrestrained, unchecked capitalism with the singular interest of making money. Lee Bollinger, president of Columbia University, avers that "climate change, issues of social justice and what globalism means for societies—all of these are raising profound questions about the nature of what the future can be." And Dean Hubbard of the business school asserts, "We are trying to come up with a framework that can be more about flourishing, and not just profit." Duh! As a critic in the project, Steven Conn, concludes, "As a historian I've heard this before, and it didn't amount to much. Institutions are very hard to change." Bollinger proposes that the business school prepares to "ask questions people did not ask about 20 or 50 years ago." Of course such a view is myopic, because many concerned people have been asking these questions for a very long time, at last since the either/or of Moses or the either/or of Jesus. Too bad the questions had not penetrated the administration of the university until now!

McCarraher goes so far as to label the Puritan

> *covenant theology of capitalism a creed whose doctrinal elements included the affirmation of wealth as a divine anointment; territorial conquest to enlarge the parameters of God's rich and faithful metropolis; a conception of the natural world as a providential storehouse of vendable wonders; and a jeremiad tradition to chastise moral failing and obscure the intractable persistence of the dilemma. (117)*

He says of this creed,

> *Under the aegis of their halfway covenant with capitalism, the Puritan errand into the wilderness became an errand into the marketplace, and American life became an experiment in Christian friendship with unrighteous Mammon. (117)*

The label *creed* is of most importance. The term means a bottom-line certitude that is beyond question and is the operating assumption for what follows derivatively. Thus the creed is a mandate for greed, whether private individual greed, the predatory practice of corporations including banks, or the insatiable appetite of aggressive states for more territory. It is all of a piece, and it is all sanctioned by the creed. It makes a nice reiteration: *creed . . . greed.*

It is obvious that a Christian creed or confession radically contradicts the creed of Mammon:

- Instead of wealth as divine anointing, we confess that *abundance is a gift from the creator God* and is to be shared with all of our fellow creatures.
- Instead of territorial expansion through conquest, debt foreclosure, or the right of eminent domain, we confess that *the territory of the vulnerable is to be respected* as a restraint against predatory seizure. The wisdom teachers echo the tenth commandment against "coveting":

Do not remove the ancient landmark
that your ancestors set up. (Prov 22:28)

Do not remove an ancient landmark
or encroach on the fields of orphans,
for their redeemer is strong;
he will plead their cause against you. (Prov 23:10–11)

- Instead of the created world as "vendable wonders," we confess that creation is *a living, breathing organism*. For that reason we know that the vendable disposal of any part of creation has important impact on every other part of creation and should be done only with care and caution.
- Instead of a jeremiad tradition that distracts and obscures, we confess that there is *real sin* against the neighbor, that *real grace* is offered to genuine repentance, and there is *real forgiveness* that we may live "a new and righteous life."

To this we may add a fifth element that belongs tacitly to McCarraher's inventory:

- Instead of enslaving debt that aims to reduce the vulnerable to debt in order to maintain a pliable work force, we confess that *our debts are forgiven* "as we forgive our debtors."

Thus it is evident with a bit of reflection that the two creeds are in contradiction to each other. It follows, as McCarraher has seen, that we have learned well the trick of both/and that covers over the severity of either/or. That both/and of *beloved community* and *capitalist foundation* is everywhere evident among us, in our institutions, in our practices, and no doubt deep in our hearts. I suspect, moreover, that the more affluent and the more sophisticated we become, the more agile we are at managing and concealing (from ourselves) the contradiction.

But such a contradiction leaves us weary and on edge. In some ways we yearn for its resolution. But while we yearn for its resolution, we also fear its exposure to light and honesty. Thus I want to reflect on Christian worship as a regular, reliable, and available venue where this most elemental contradiction can be processed with some honesty, called by name, and seen for what it is when it is seen clearly free of ideological palaver.

The Christian creed, in its various articulations, is the subject and pervasive theme of Christian worship. That creed/confession, as we have seen, touches all the facets of that contradiction with its selfish wealth, territorial ambitions, vendable wonders, and jeremiads, plus ruthless indebtedness. The force of the creed of capitalism is present every time we meet. And the counterpoints and antidotes of the gospel are also present every time we meet: prayer, singing, generous sharing, offers of God's grace, honest sin and forgiveness of debts, exposition, and proclamation. All of that is operative every time we meet. The meeting is first of all about the claim and structure of creed and confession. We do that in our praise and in our prayers when we are together. We sing of the wonder of the abundance by the grace of God. In prayer we present ourselves as glad recipients of this alternative world that is, in a glimpse, beyond our fatiguing domestication. And then in Scripture and sermon, there is a chance to consider the contradiction that surges among us. Attention to Scripture and brave exposition in sermon together present to us both the force of the contradiction and the wonder of the God of grace to override that contradiction.

While the articulation of the claim of our confession or creed is urgent, the true work of ministry is in the processing of the contradiction. Almost none of us is open to radical abrupt change or transformation. Better the work is slow nurture. But imagine the reality! Liberal Christians and conservative Christians all together in a meeting where we acknowledge together the contradiction that besets us all. With patience and perseverance, through this regular meeting (as almost nowhere else) we have opportunity to "grow in grace" to relinquish the dominant creed of capitalism, and to regard our money, our lives, and our neighbors very differently.

I am convinced that it does little good in the congregation to harp on stewardship. The work is to invite down into the hidden contradiction that immobilizes and assaults us, and to be in a posture for change, gratitude, renewal, and forgiveness. We are not meant to be beset by creeds that are not in sync with our true selves. We are meant, rather, to be *forgiven, emancipated selves* in a community of *the forgiven and emancipated*, freed to live a life that decisively rejects, defies, and refuses the dominant creed of our society.

We are cast, among many other roles, as the well-known "rich young ruler" who turned away from Jesus because "he had many possessions" (Mark 10:22). But the sad departure of the rich man isn't the end of the story. The confrontation with the rich young ruler and his departure is, for Jesus and his disciples, an opportunity for critical reflection and teaching. Jesus draws the conclusion from the departure of the rich man that our defining contradiction is very difficult (vv. 23–25). His disciples get the point; they know that they are caught in the same dilemma; they are hopeless and lost. But then this from the master:

> *For mortals it is impossible, but not for God; for God all things are possible. (v. 27)*

It is *impossible* to extricate ourselves from this defining contradiction. But Jesus, to the contrary, declares *the possibility for God.* It is the God of the gospel who extricates us from such a powerful dilemma.

So focus yet again on the gospel possibility of worship. Our work in ministry is to process the contradiction and to embrace what we judge to be impossible. That impossibility from God does happen. It happens by song and prayer and proclamation and study. When it happens, it is a gift to be lived out in gladness. It is, to be sure, very upstream and against all odds for all of us, but it is possible. It is *our work*, and *the work of God* who is in and through and among us!

> *Work out your own salvation with fear and trembling, for it is God who is at work in you, enabling you both to will and to work for his good pleasure. (Phil 2:12–13)*

Part V

NEW EARTH

Growing up in a farming community gave me a strong work ethic. I think it gave me deep moral grounding. Because it was a world in which you were as good as your word. I think it also gave me great impetus to study. Because I thought I don't want to do this, the rest of my life. I had these two summers in college in which I plowed corn and bailed hay and I modestly resented having to do that—it wasn't satisfying to me personally, because I never quite knew what I was doing. I never quite knew if I had it right. Because the attitude of people that you work on the farm is where you either know how to do this or you'll figure it out so just go do it so. The land was creation. One had this sense with farmers that they had a huge respect for the growing season and impact of weather and the fact that we are, in many ways, dependent on what's dealt to us seasonally, which I suppose is a great warning against self-sufficiency. That part really continues to be important to me. I think that's kind of important to see: the natural processes of growth and reproduction and all that stuff. When I began in Old Testament study the big accent was God's mighty deeds in history. And nature or creation was neglected partly. That was because of Barth's aversion to natural theology. So my book on the land was my own growing awareness that our life of faith cannot be reduced to a series of historical moments. But there is a spacious continuity about land and about the place where God has put us. So that's the argument that I tried to make in that book. It was my effort to get beyond what I thought was an overaccent on isolated moments of miracles and that the great miracle is the life-giving processes of creation. I don't think I saw that very clearly, but that's what I was trying to get to.

15

TRACTOR

Icon of Predatory Development

THIS IS A report on a surprising convergence in my reading. Three authors, from different times and in very different contexts, all regard "he tractor as a symbol of the destructive power of industrial development that endangers traditional, viable forms of common human life.

1. I remembered that John Steinbeck, long ago in *The Grapes of Wrath*, had featured the tractor as a symbol of such menace to the vulnerable Okies in his narrative. Tractors are the implement whereby a farmer can cultivate and manage larger acreage, which in turn caused the displacement of many of Steinbeck's Okies:

> *And the men looked up for a second, and the smolder of pain was in their eyes. We got to get off. A tractor and a superintendent. Like factories . . . the tractors came over the roads and into the fields, great crawlers moving like insects, having the incredible strength of insects. They crawled over the ground, laying the track and rolling on it and picking it up. Diesel tractors, puttering while they stood idle; they thundered when they moved, and then settled down to a droning roar. Snub-nosed monsters, raising the dust and sticking their snouts into it, straight down the country, across the country, through fences, through dooryards, in and out of gullies in straight lines. They did not run on the ground,*

> *but on their own roadbeds. They ignored hills and gulches, water courses, fences, houses . . . A twitch at the controls could swerve the cat', but the driver's hands could not twitch because the monster that built the tractor, the monster that sent the tractor out, had somehow got into the driver's hands, into his brain and muscle, had goggled him and muzzled him—goggled his mind, muzzled his speech, goggled his perception, muzzled his protest. He could not see the land as it was, he could not smell the land as it smelled; his feet did not stamp the clods or feel the warmth and power of the earth. . . . The driver sat in his iron seat and he was proud of the straight lines he did not will, proud of the tractor he did not own or love, proud of the power he could not control. . . . The land bore under iron, and under iron gradually died; for it was not loved or hated, it had no prayers or curses. (Penguin, 1939, 44–47)*

The tractor evoked the futile violent resistance of the Okies:

> *Well, they was gonna stick her out when the bank came to tractorin' off the place. Your grampa stood out here with a rifle, an' he blowed the headlights off that cat', but she came on just the same. Your grampa didn't wanta kill the guy drivin' that cat', an' that was Willy Feeley, an' Willy knowed it, so he jus' come on, an' bumped the hell outa the house, an' give her a shake like a dog shakes a rat. Well, it took somepin outa Tom. Kinda got into 'im. He ain't been the same ever since. (58–59)*

But Steinbeck's narrator knows that there are limits to what a tractor can accomplish. There is costly pushback against its aggressive gains:

> *And the great owners who must lose their land in an upheaval, the great owners with access to history, with eyes*

> *to read history and to know the great fact; when property accumulates into too few hands it is taken away. And that companion fact: when a majority of the people are hungry and cold they will take by force what they need. And the little screaming fact that sounds through all history; repression works only to strengthen and knit the repressed. The great owners ignored the three cries of history. . . .*
>
> *The tractors which throw men out of work, the belt lines which carry loads, the machines which produce, all were increased; and more and more families scampered on the highways, looking for crumbs from the great holdings, lusting after the land beside the roads. The great owners formed associations for protection and they met to discuss ways to intimidate, to kill, to gas. And always they were in fear of a principal—three hundred thousand—if they ever move under a leader—the end. Three hundred thousand, hungry and miserable; if they ever know themselves, the land will be theirs and all the gas, all the rifles in the world won't stop them. And the great owners, who had become through their holdings both more and less than men, ran to their destruction, and used every means that in the long run would destroy them. Every little means, every violence, every raid on a Hooverville, every deputy swaggering through a ragged camp put off the day a little and cemented the inevitability of the day. (306–7)*

The three cries of history will weep to retaliation and to restoration. The narrator judges that the reversal will be "inevitable."

When we read these lines, we are made aware that Steinbeck wrote in the midst of the depression. His reference to Hooverville locates him rather precisely. It was a time of desperation and despair; but it was also a time of possibility with the organizing power of labor. At our distance from Steinbeck, this belated hope of reversal strikes one as optimistic, because such possibilities do not so clearly appear on the horizon now. But Steinbeck could anticipate that in their desperation, the three hundred thousand displaced could make claims and succeed in them. Thus he asserts that the tractor, as icon of destructive development, could not be the ultimate arbiter of human destiny. Even then, however, Steinbeck sees clearly that the tractor was indeed a destroyer of human community, human possibility, and human destiny. The famous ending of his tale is an insistence that human mercy, care, and solidarity constitute the ultimate truth of the human condition (580–81).

2. The long-running passionate testimony of Wendell Berry comes powerfully in the wake of Steinbeck. In his best-known novel, *Jayber Crow: A Novel; The Life Story of Jayber Crow, Barber, of the Port William Membership as Written by Himself*, Berry (surely with a tacit nod to Steinbeck) presents Athey aka "Mr. Keith," and his wife Della, as an embodiment of an agrarian way of life that lives from the land and back to the land. In what I think are Berry's best lines he writes of Della and Athey,

> *They were a sight to see, Della and Athey were, in their vigorous years. They had about them a sort of intimation of abundance, as though, like magicians, they might suddenly fill the room with potatoes, onions, turnips, summer squashes, and ears of corn drawn from their pockets. Their place had about it that quality of bottomless fecundity, its richness both in evidence and in reserve. . . .*
>
> *Their life is marked by the abundance of a small farm that has been properly cared for. Athey can say, "Wherever I look, I want to see more than I need." (Penguin, 2000, 181)*

Athey is contrasted to his son-in-law Troy. This is how Athey's farm looks to Troy:

In coming to the Keith place, he [Troy] had come into an order that perhaps he did not even recognize. Over a long time, the coming and passing of several generations, the old farm had settled into its patterns and cycles of work—its annual plowing moving from field to field; its animals arriving by birth or purchase, feeding and growing, thriving and departing. Its patterns and cycles were virtually the farm's own understanding of what it was doing, of what it could do without diminishment. This order was not unintelligent or rigid. It tightened and slackened, shifted and changed in response to the markets and the weather. The Depression had changed it somewhat, and so had the war. But through all changes so far, the farm had endured. Its cycles of cropping and grazing, thought and work, were articulations of its wish to cohere and to last. The farm, so to speak, desired all of its lives to flourish. (182)

Athey is insistent on the matter:

Athey was not exactly, or not only, what is called a "landowner." He was the farm's farmer, but also its creature and belonging. He lived its life, and it lived his; he knew that, of the two lives, his was meant to be the smaller and the shorter. (182)

That war of flourishing concerned "the entire old fabric of family work and exchanges of work among neighbors." (183)

Athey's farming practice is balanced, and he is willing to settle for modest but adequate productivity:

The law of the farm was in the balance between crops (including hay and pasture) and livestock. The farm would have no more livestock than it could carry without strain.

> *No more land would be plowed for grain crops than could be fertilized with manure from the animals. No more grain would be grown than the animals could eat. Except in cases of unexpected surpluses or deficiencies, the farm did not sell or buy livestock feed. "I mean my grain and hay to leave my place on foot," Athey liked to say. This was a conserving principle; it strictly limited both the amount of land that would be plowed and the amount of supplies that would have to be bought. Athey did not save money at the expense of his farm or his family, but he looked upon spending it as a last resort; he spent no more than was necessary, and he hated debt. (185)*

But Troy fully intends otherwise. He is impatient with the old ways of his father-in-law. He does not at all understand that he belongs to the farm. He understands only that the farm belongs to him, and he can work to make it maximally productive. He intends, by plowing up more land, using commercial fertilizer, and in general exploiting the land, that he will produce more.

The potent symbol of Troy's perception is the tractor:

> *The government was teaching a new way of farming in night courses for the veterans. Tractors and other farm machines were all of a sudden available as never before, and farmhands were scarcer than before. And so we began a process of cause-and-effect that is hard to understand clearly, even looking back. Did the machines displace the people from the farms, or were the machines drawn onto the farms because people were already leaving to take up wage work in factories and the building trades and such? Both I think. (183)*

For Troy, his life seems dominated by the tractor, which gave him an awesome sense of power:

> *Troy liked to climb on the tractor, open the throttle, and just go, whatever the time of day, his mind invested with the machine's indifference to weariness and to features of the landscape . . . and Troy felt also that he had a lot to prove. As it turned out, he would have more reason every year to feel so. Year by year, he increased his rented acreage elsewhere, thereby increasing the pressure on Athey to give him more say-so over the Keith place. For Troy would one day farm that farm, and Athey wanted his interest there. Little by little, he began giving way to Troy's wants and ideas, and the old pattern of the farm began to give way. (186)*

Berry sees that the dispute between father-in-law and son-in-law is defining and elementary:

> *And so the farm came under the influence of a new pattern, and this was the pattern of a fundamental disagreement such as it had never seen before. It was a disagreement about time and money and the use of the world. . . . The conflicts were inescapable, were just there as part and parcel of the farm and what was happening on it. The work of the farm now went on at two different rates of speed and power and endurance. It became hard to cooperate, not because cooperation was impossible, but because the tractor and the teams embodied two different kinds of will, almost two different intentions. It was a difference of character and history. (186)*

This shift of perception and practice from one generation to the next has been a major theme for Berry's work. His more recent work, as in *A World Lost*, has taken the tone of an elegy for a world lost and a struggle for the old agrarian way as defeated. One can notice that there is not, for Berry as for Steinbeck, the prospect of a reversal. We may hope—and wish—that Steinbeck's hope can prevail. But for Berry the struggle for the old pattern of farming has been lost. In the process of the victory of the tractor, the land has changed in its character. It is no longer a habitat for intergenerational well-being. Now it is a commodity designed to produce greater commodities. The old notion of farmers belonging to the land has been forfeited. Industrialization wins!

3. A third articulation of the same crisis comes, for me, from a surprising source, an author not yet so well known. Abdelraham Munif has written a series of books that reflect on the coming of American business interests to the Arabian Peninsula in search of oil. Munif writes from the perspective of his own people, namely, the vulnerable Arab population that is the victim of the Western incursion into their land, often with the collusion of their own governments.

Through the course of his novel, *Cities of Salt* (Random House, 1984), Munif describes the aggressive way in which Western seekers of oil assaulted Arab culture, devastated their oasis, which is the locus of the narrative, and settled into air-conditioned quarters while local workers had none. He portrays the sad scene in which his lead character, Miteb al-Hathal, grieves the loss of his oasis and his way of life: "I'm sorry, Wadi al-Uyoun . . . I'm sorry."

And then he writes,

> *This was the final, insane, accursed proclamation that everything had come to an end. For anyone who remembers those long-ago days, when a place called Wadi al-Uyoun used to exist, and a man name Miteb al-Hathal, and a brook, and trees, and a community of people used to exist, the three things that still break his heart in recalling those days are the tractors which attacked the orchards like ravenous wolves, tearing up*

> *the trees and throwing them to the earth one after another, and leveled all orchards between the brook and the fields. After destroying the first grove of trees, the tractors turned to the next with the same bestial voracity and uprooted them. The trees shook violently and groaned before falling, cried for help, wailed, panicked, called out in helpless pain and then fell entreatingly to the ground, as if trying to snuggle into the earth to grow and spring forth alive again. (107)*

It is like a refrain that hums to the sound of the tractor:

- Tractor—orchards attached by ravenous wolves;
- Tractor—trees torn up and thrown to the ground;
- Tractor—orchards leveled between brook and fields.

And as the landscape goes, so goes human habitation as well.

It is no wonder that these pages end with a glance at the "maddened machines," and then grief. Munif reports on the response of Miteb al-Hathal to the ruin:

> *They said it was the first time in their lives they had ever seen a man like Miteb al- Hathal cry. He could not stop crying, but he did so silently. He was perfectly silent. He did not say one word. He did not curse. Not a single sound or word escaped his lips; he shed his tears, unashamed and unafraid, but not proud either. He looked quietly through his tears at the whole wadi and shook his head. (106–7)*

Then he makes his silent preparations:

> *He worked calmly, readying everything he needed, without looking at anyone, without hearing a single word they said. He still had tearstains on his face but he did not cry, and*

> *when he had finished preparing everything he gathered up is rifle and waterskin and mounted his Omani camel. He looked at them all, at each of their faces in turn as if memorizing them, and when he had scrutinized them all he kicked the camel's side, and she trembled as she reared up and stood. Miteb al-Hathal rose on her back like a huge tent, and he looked like a cloud, and when he sped off he looked like a white bird. He faded from sight and grew smaller, dwindled and then disappeared. (107)*

He left! There was nothing there for him anymore. His world had been lost, taken away by the tractor. The departure of Miteb al-Hathal resonates with the elegy of Berry for a life—and a way of life—that has been negated by the machine.

Full disclosure: I have "seen both sides." In high school in Blackburn, Missouri, I cultivated corn with a team of horses. In college I cultivated corn with a tractor in Beaver Crossing, Nebraska. Both tasks for me produced great anxiety.

It is far too late to object to the tractor as a farm implement. But for Steinbeck, Berry, and Munif the tractor is something other than just a farm implement. It is an icon and metaphor for the greedy rush of development, for the urge to expansive power and wealth. The tractor represents all of the violent urges to obliterate long-running cultures that violate neighborhoods, and deny neighbors the slow, daily practice of generosity and compassion. It may be that we end in grief alongside Berry and Munif. Or it may be that we make fresh resolve for practice and policy that will not yield to such antineighborly urges, and so perform Steinbeck's hope.

We are, perhaps, watching the final rundown of the Industrial Revolution. We are reaping what we have unwittingly sown in terms of environmental crisis and the exhaustion of the growth economy. As we remember what we have lost, we watch as the violent urge continues to advance. That violent urge will only be contained by a recovery, restoration, and rehabilitation of a neighborly economy. That of course is what our faith tradition has been at since the initial effort of Moses. The Torah—and Jesus as child of the Torah—understood that neighborliness counts decisively. Thus we stand, as we always do—before the great either/or of prophetic imagination:

> *Thus says the LORD: Do not let the wise boast in their wisdom, do not let the mighty boast in their might, do not let the wealthy boast in their wealth; but let those who boast in this, that they understand and know me, that I am the LORD; I act with steadfast love, justice, and righteousness in the earth, for in these things I delight, says the LORD. (Jer 9:23–24).*

The accumulation of *wisdom, power, and wealth* works its ruinous way. But then, we may be grateful, in turn to Steinbeck, Berry, and Munif, for their bold exhibit of the unimaginable costs of industrial "progress." The tractor is king. For that reason lament is in order; but then, this is our time for a way more excellent than wisdom, wealth, and power. The more excellent way, as always, concerns *steadfast love, justice, and righteousness.*

18

TREES

Signals of Hope and Defiance

THIS IS AN unabashed commendation of a book. The book by Franck Prevot is entitled *Wangari Maathai: The Woman Who Planted Millions of Trees* (Charlesbridge, 2015).This children's book, with its winsome art work, tells the story of Wangari Maathai, a Kenyan woman who learned from her mother that "a tree is worth more than its wood." As she grew up she became aware that her black African people were deprived of much of their land for agriculture. She saw the devastation of the forests as her country gained independence from Britain. In the face of all the deforestation, her mother taught her:

> *A tree is a treasure that provides shade, fruit, pure air, and nesting places for birds, and that pulses with the vitality of life. Trees are hideouts for insects and provide inspiration for poets. A tree is a little bit of the future. (21)*

In response to the destruction of deforestation that she could observe, Maathai organized the Green Belt Movement to encourage villagers to plant many, many trees. She encountered much opposition from business interests and from the authoritarian government of Daniel arap Moi. She was imprisoned by the government for her oppositional stance, but slowly she was able to gain public support for her democratic vision of society. Her great courage led not only to many trees, but to the flourishing of democracy in her home country of Kenya. It is clear that her story is one that our children and grandchildren urgently need to hear, a story of courage in devotion to the well-being of the earth and its creaturely population.

This story, told artfully and accessibly, has led me to think about trees and the role they play in the Bible for a viable creation (and a viable economy). That crucial role played by trees has been played since the appearance of trees on the third day of creation (Gen 1:11–13). This is some of what I learned about trees in the Bible:

1. In the Torah provision of Deuteronomy 20:19–20 fruit trees are given explicit protection, because their presence and flourishing are indispensable for the well-being of creaturely life:

   If you besiege a town for a long time, making war against it in order to take it, you must not destroy its trees by wielding an ax against them. Although you may take food from them, you must not cut them down. Are trees in the field human beings that they should come under siege from you? (v. 19)

   This Torah provision, I suggest, is closest to the core passion of Wangari Maathai who understood ecological balance. In the Torah provision tree protection is from the devastation of war when trees could be cut down for siege weapons. Alongside the risks of war, a greater risk among us is the threat of developers who are quite willing to devastate trees in the interest of making money. The Torah regulation eagerly vetoes a trade-off of trees for money!
2. In the doxological tradition of Israel, trees are reckoned as lively creatures and not simply inanimate objects waiting to be exploited. As lively creatures, trees are gladly included in the joyous praise of Israel to the creator:

Let the heavens be glad, and let the earth rejoice;
let the sea roar, and all that fills it;

let the field exult, and everything in it.
Then shall all the trees of the forest sing for joy
before the LORD; for he is coming,
for he is coming to judge the earth. (Ps 96:11–13)

Praise the LORD from the earth,
you sea monsters and all deeps,
fire and hail, snow and frost,
stormy wind fulfilling his command!
Mountains and all hills,
fruit trees and all cedars!
Wild animals and all cattle,
creeping things and flying birds! (Ps 148:7–10)

Sing, O heavens, for the LORD has done it;
shout, O depths of the earth;
break forth into singing, O mountains,
O forest, and every tree in it! (Isa 44:23)

The mountains and the hills before you
shall burst into song,
and all the trees of the field shall clap their hands. (Isa 55:12)

These lyrical lines trace out the "Social Life of Trees" as creatures in full engagement with their creator. Or perhaps better, "The Doxological Life of Trees"!

All the trees of the field shall know
that I am the LORD.
I bring low the high tree,
I make high the low tree;
I dry up the green tree
and make the dry tree flourish.

I the LORD have spoken;
I will accomplish it. (Ezek 17:24)

3. Like everything else in creation, trees can be distorted and put to ignoble use. Isaiah can describe with some ironic specificity how trees can be deployed for idol worship by addressing them as targets of prayers:

He cuts down cedars or chooses a holm tree or an oak and lets it grow strong among the trees of the forest. He plants a cedar and the rain nourishes it. Then it can be used as fuel. Part of it he takes and warms himself; he kindles a fire and bakes bread. Then he makes a god and worships it, makes it a carved image and bows down before it. Half of it he burns in the fire; over this half he roasts meat, eats it and is satisfied. He also warms himself and says, "Ah, I am warm, I can feel the fire!" The rest of it he makes into a god, his idol, bows down to it and worships it; he prays to it and says, "Save me, for you are my god!" (Isa 44:14–18)

This process of "god-making" shows how a creature of God is turned into a god. It is no wonder that the prophet ends his critique with an ironic rhetorical question:

Is not this thing in my right hand a fraud? (Isa 44:20)

Such inanimate objects of wood are, like the greater idolatrous designs of silver and gold, incapable of transformative action:

They have mouths, but they do not speak;
they have eyes, but they do not see;
they have ears, but they do not hear,
and there is no breath in their mouths. (Ps 135:16–17)

The point is compellingly reiterated by Jeremiah:

For the customs of the peoples are false;
a tree from the forest is cut down,
and worked with an ax by the hands of an artisan;
people deck it with silver and gold;
they fasten it with hammer and nails
so that it cannot move.
Their idols are like scarecrows in a cucumber field,
and they cannot speak;
they have to be carried,
for they cannot walk.
Do not be afraid of them,
for they cannot do evil,
nor is it in them to do good. (Jer 10:3–5)

Trees have a major role to play in the well-being of creation. But posturing as gods is not one of them.

4. At the opposite pole from "making gods," King Solomon misperceived trees by seeing them simply as materials for construction that would in turn exhibit his great wealth. His narrative is permeated with mention of wood used in his extensive constructions including his temple:

Hiram sent word to Solomon, "I have heard the message that you have sent to me; I will fulfill all your needs in the matter of cedar and cypress timber. . . . *The entrance for the middle story was on the south side of the house; one went up by winding stairs to the middle story, and from the middle story to the third. So he built the house, and finished it; he roofed the house with* beams and planks of cedar. *He built the structure against the whole house, each story five cubits high, and it was joined to the house with*

> timbers of cedar. . . . *He lined the walls of the house on the inside with* boards of cedar, *from the floor of the house to the rafters of the ceiling, he covered them on the inside with wood; and he covered the floor of the house with* boards of cypress. . . . *He built the House of the Forest of Lebanon one hundred cubits long, fifty cubits wide, and thirty cubits high, built on four rows of* cedar pillars, *with* cedar beams *on the pillars. . . . He made the Hall of the Throne where he was to pronounce judgment, the Hall of Justice, covered with* cedar *from floor to floor. . . . King Hiram of Tyre having supplied Solomon with* cedar and cypress timber *and gold, as much as he desired, King Solomon gave to Hiram twenty cities in the land of Galilee. (1 Kings 5:8, 6:8–10, 15, 7:2, 7, 9:11)*

While Solomon may not have stooped to the practice of wooden idols, he clearly had no passion for trees as an important marker of the creaturely order willed by the creator, and given back to God in glad praise. Solomon had nothing more than an instrumental interest in trees, as he had for everything else on which he could lay his hands, including even his own people and the women he appropriated. Everything—including trees—was nothing more to him than usable, expendable commodities.

5. Given the twin temptations of *wood for worship* and *wood for commerce*, we might expect the complete exhaustion of trees. There is, however, witness to the contrary amid the poetic lament of Job. Job makes a contrast between trees and dispensable nobodies like himself. He says of himself and other mortals:

But mortals die, and are laid low;
humans expire, and where are they?

As waters fail from a lake,
and a river wastes away and dries up,
so mortals lie down and do not rise again;
until the heavens are no more, they will not awake
or be roused out of their sleep. (Job 14:10–12)

Job has concluded, "When you're dead, you're dead!" But trees, by contrast, can rise again:

For there is hope for a tree,
if it is cut down, that it will sprout again,
and that its shoots will not cease.
Though its root grows old in the earth,
and its stump dies in the ground,
yet at the scent of water it will bud
and put forth branches like a young plant. (Job 14:7–9)

Trees can be restored to life; all it takes is the revivifying aroma of water, a fact anyone knows who has engaged in the hopeless task of trying to eliminate unwanted sprouts. We may take these words of Job as a compelling response to the *tree-exhausting work* of *idol making* and the *commercial expenditure of wood.* Trees possess the vitality of creatureliness given them by the creator. As trees have hope, so they may also be a source of hope amid a world seemingly done to death by deforestation.

There can be no doubt that Wangari Maathai had all of this in purview intuitively. She knew that planting trees was an act of hope in a society that had suffered so much at the hands of a rapacious authoritarian regime. She knew that planting trees would yield energy for taking democratic risks. She knew that nurturing care for the "natural" world would bring with it generative care for the public, political-economic process of common life as well.

Of course there is much more to the life and work of Maathai than can be included in this children's book. She lectured in veterinarian anatomy at the University of Nairobi. Her work with the Kenyan Red Cross Society led her to involvement in the UN Program of Environmentalism. She linked her concern for the unemployed in her society with environmental needs that resulted in her planting trees. She worked at Envirocare, which led to her first UN conference in 1976. In the next year she led a bold procession into downtown Nairobi to Kumukunji Park, where they planted seven trees, thus initiating what became the Green Belt Movement.

In 1979 she became chair of the National Council of Women of Kenya, an umbrella organization for a host of women's organizations. She rose to great prominence and so became a leader in resistance to Daniel arap Moi, the authoritarian president of Kenya. She became a point person in resistance and was variously harassed by the government and the police. Through her persistence the government of Moi was defeated. In 2003 she entered into the newly formed government as Assistant Minister for Environmental and Natural Resources. In 2004 she received the Nobel Peace Prize. Until her death in 2011 she continued to flourish in ever more influential posts to advance both democracy and environmentalism. She was a relentless, brave witness to the conviction that our public political processes can indeed serve the common good.

I submit that beginning with this children's book, Wangari Maathai merits our close study concerning how a life propelled toward the common good can make a decisive difference in the life of the world. She began as a vulnerable uncredentialed woman; she ended with stark and stunning accomplishments for the wellbeing of her people.

It is not too early for our kids to learn about state violence that aims at control and private wealth.

It is not too early for our kids to learn that brave lives lived to the contrary can matter decisively.

It is not too early for our kids to learn that political issues of justice are deeply linked to environmental issues of creaturely viability.

It is not too early for our kids to learn that brave action grounded in hope for the future, even against great odds, serves to create alternative futures.

Martin Luther was famously asked what he would do if he knew the world was ending. He famously answered, "I would plant a tree." He would plant a tree as an act of defiant hope. Wangari Maathai has gone beyond Luther's subjunctive "I would" to actually do the planting. In doing so, she eventually defeated the forces of oppression. She not only marked the end of that world of violence, but she opened a way for an alternative future in her society. A children's book is a good way to start a conversation about hope and defiance, about faith that is

> *the assurance of things hoped for, the conviction of things not seen. (Heb 11:1)*

Her brave hope was an act of defiance, a refusal to accept political-social arrangements that seemed to be firmly and permanently established. In her hope, she knew better!

17

MAPPING

I LOVE MAPS and mapping. My early most durable memory of maps comes from my wee rural grade school in Blackburn, Missouri. In geography class in seventh grade (or so), we had weekly "map study." Each pupil had a map of the world; our teacher would call out a state or a nation or a larger city. We would see who could identify it first. My brother Ed, a year older than I, was in the same geography class. He and I gamed the system a bit by each of us taking one hemisphere. In that way, we could often be the first to identify the named place.

I have thought about that mapping exercise when I read Jo Guldi's magisterial book, *The Long Land War: The Global Struggle for Occupancy Rights* (Yale, 2021). The book concerns the landless around the world. At the end of her book, Guldi identifies two strategies whereby landless people may acquire land. One such strategy is the exercise of squatters' rights whereby landless folk simply take over space that others claim to own. The other strategy she explores is "mapping." I will return to her study a bit later. Guldi shows that the word *mapping* is a gerund that functions as a verb before it can be a noun. Mapping is a unilateral activity that is shaped by and reflective of the exercise of power, control and, often, wealth.

For now I will begin with a consideration of mapping in the Old Testament, the drawing of boundaries, and the claiming of territories. Already with the Abraham narrative, Israel has a map of the land promised to it:

> *To your descendants I give this land, from the river of Egypt to the great river, the river Euphrates, the land of Kenites, the*

> *Kenizzites, the Kadmonites, the Hittites, the Perizzites, the Rephaim, the Amorites, the Canaanites, the Girgashites, and the Jebusites. (Gen 15:18–21)*

Well, this is not yet a map, but an expansive imaginative sketch of the land of promise of God at its most expansive. The maps to come later in Israel are all contained within this expansive vision.

When we get more specific I can identify three maps in the Israelite tradition concerning the land of promise.

1. The narrative account of Joshua 13:1–17:18, with the addenda of 18:1–22:34, constitutes a first map of Israel as the land of promise. In this authorizing address to Joshua the tradition traces out the "inheritance of the tribes of Israel." This mapping imagines that the tribal structure of Israel was clear, intact, traceable, and with boundaries that could be clearly and firmly delineated. We may doubt that the facts on the ground concerning both tribal structure and boundaries were nearly as clean and tidy as suggested here. In this mapping each tribe is allotted a territory. The exception is the tribe of Levi; it is noted repeatedly that the tribe of Levi receives no such inheritance (Josh 13:14; 14:3; 18:7). In chapter 21, other provision is made for the Levites.

   This mapping comes in the wake of the forcible conquest of the land in earlier chapters in Joshua. While the narrative features a conquest, I find it most compelling to interpret the text according to the "peasant revolt" hypothesis of Norman Gottwald. According to that rendition, the "conquest" was an overthrow of top-down exploitative ("Canaanite") authority by the assertion of the rights of the rural landless peasants who lived in a subsistence economy. This narrative is honest enough to acknowledge that the "revolt" was not everywhere successful and complete, so that "Canaanites" continued to be present amid the population.

Joshua is authorized in a direct address from YHWH to apportion the land:

Now therefore divide this land for an inheritance to the nine tribes and the half-tribe of Manasseh. (Josh 13:7)

This verse that pertains to the West Jordan is followed in verse 8 with provision for the tribes to the east of the Jordan. The allotment thus is done with the authority of Joshua, but with the positive sanction of YHWH, who is the Lord of the land and the guarantor of the land rights of the peasants.

Special provision is made for Caleb, who, along with Joshua, was the most zealous about taking the land (Josh 4:6–13). While the tribes are treated with equity, Caleb has a peculiar claim that is honored in the land apportionment. It is worth noting that daughters can have as much claim on the land as sons (Josh 17:3–6; see Num 36).

The narrative is eager to assert that the apportionment of the land was complete, final, and settled:

Thus the whole congregation of the Israelites assembled at Shiloh, and set up the tent of meeting there. The land lay subdued before them. (18:1)

But clearly the tradition recognizes that the settlement of the land was an ongoing process of negotiation and conflict. The claim that the occupation of the land by the peasants was settled and closed is an ideological claim that cannot possibly square with the facts on the ground.

The notion of finality is further enforced by the act of writing. Once written, the land arrangement seems to be permanent and uncontested. Or as my German forebears could say, *Es steht geschreiben*. Such writing is an ideological act that can only "stick" in reality if there is a general acceptance of the claim. Here much of it seems to have remained contested. Writing is an act that makes ownership appear to be legitimate and beyond contestation.

It will be noted that this mapping never pauses to consider the land claims of the previous occupants. Read according to the peasant revolt hypothesis, the aggressive subsistence peasants never paused to consider the "rights" of the Canaanite landowners before them. It is the way of land-hungry peasants to disregard any former land arrangements that had been predatory or exclusionary. Thus the "land promise" made to Father Abraham is brought to fruition through a combination of coercive violence and ideological preemption. In making its claim to the land, however, Israel readily glosses over coercive violence, and rests its claim in the simple elemental assurance that the Lord of the land intended the landless peasants to have the land, fully settled in security:

> *Thus the LORD gave to Israel all the land that he swore to their ancestors that he would give them; and having taken possession of it, they settled there. And the LORD gave them rest on every side just as he had sworn to their ancestors; not one of all their enemies had withstood them for the LORD had given all their enemies into their hands. Not one of all the good promises that the LORD had made to the house of Israel had failed; all came to pass. (Josh 21:43–45)*

The final phrase in Hebrew is terse: "All came." "All arrived." The geographical reality is a perfect, effective fit with the promissory decree of YHWH. Such a claim is free to disregard the dispute that always belongs to land ownership. The summary is a compelling cover over such socioeconomic realities. God is faithful!

2. A second very different mapping of the land is offered in 1 Kings 4:7–19. This is a mapping of Solomon's tax districts. Verse 7 makes clear that the purpose of these tax districts is the systematic collection of revenue (agricultural produce) to support the grandiose, indulgent life of Solomon and his royal entourage. (On such indulgence see 1 Kings 4:22–23.) It strikes one immediately that here there is no mention of divine allotment or approval. Thus we can readily imagine that this map was drawn up in an administrative office of the king. This mapping pays no attention to local tradition or to conventional tribal claims. We may notice that in verse 13 we are given a glimpse into the systemic disregard for social differentiation, as lumped together are village (*hawwah*), region (*hebel*) and "great cities" (*'urim gedoloth*) with walls and bronze bars. Nothing of local or social differences matter at all. All that matters was that the revenues were available and could be confiscated. (It is to be noticed that in 1 Kings 12:1–19, in the wake of Solomon's death, it is the aggressive predatory tax system of Solomon's regime that caused the revolt of the North, and the loss of territory for the Jerusalem regime. The predatory flavor of this taxing system is perhaps reinforced with the report in verses 11 and 15 that Abenabinadab and Ahimaaz, tax collectors in two districts, were sons-in-law of the king. It is likely they had joined "the family business" of extractive tax collection, a phrasing that suggests something like a mob operation. In any case, the capacity to preside over a tax district was lucrative indeed! This mapping surely reflects a political economy that had no interest in linking economic reality to old tribal realities or to the covenantal claims of YHWH. This is a map that reflects the raw, shameless exercise of power whereby "neighbors" are recast simply as sources of revenue. We may indeed be surprised that it was not until after Solomon's death that a revolt emerged. But then, under a strong regime, the peasants may wait a long time

(or never!) before mobilizing effective opposition. The mapping in the book of Joshua can still imagine a community of neighborly tribes. By the time of Solomon such a community of neighbors has become a forgotten legacy.

We may notice that these two mappings, of Joshua's tribes and Solomon's tax districts, bespeak two ways of organizing social power. We may take a glimpse at the narrative of Naboth's vineyard in 1 Kings 21. The two protagonists in the narrative, Naboth and Ahab, are dramatic representatives of these two mappings. Whereas Naboth depended on and appealed to the old tribal "inheritance," Ahab appealed to a notion of land as a commodity. Joshua's map is concerned with inheritance. Solomon's map is preoccupied with commodity. In the short run, Ahab and the commodity map prevails. Except that Elijah, rooted in the old covenantal tradition, has a final say in the narrative (1 Kings 21:17–19).

3. third map from the Old Testament that I cite is in Ezekiel 47:13–48:29. This is an anticipatory sketch of tribal Israel when it is restored after the exile. The prophet imagines a reallotment of territory by the tribes, not unlike the earlier work of Joshua. The expanse of this restoration of Israel will be according to the vision of Greater Israel promised to Abraham that stretches from the Great Sea far to the north and as far south as Egypt. The most important feature of this map is that it imagines Israel in perfect symmetry clustered around the holiness of Jerusalem and its restored temple. Notable is the provision that the restored community will now include "aliens" (*gr*) as well as citizens" (*zrh*):

You shall allot it as an inheritance for yourselves and for the aliens who reside among you and have begotten children among you. They shall be to you as citizens of Israel; with you they shall be allotted an inheritance among the tribes of

> *Israel. In whatever tribe aliens reside, there you shall assign them their inheritance, says the Lord. (Ezek 47:22–23)*

The key marker of restored Israel is its holiness that will correspond to the holy God who dwells at the center of Israel in the sanctuary, whose gates shall "remain shut" so that the Holy One will never again depart (44:1–2). Thus the final word of Ezekiel assures God's presence in the holy place: "The Lord is There" (48:35). This mapping of Israel is quite indifferent to any historical complication or any sociopolitical, economic inconvenience. All that counts is the holiness that marks the entire life of Israel that eventuates in an ordered, symmetrical, undisturbed existence that befits the serene solemnity of the priests and the holy space over which they preside.

One is immediately struck by how very different the interests and production of these three maps are. They represent in turn the interests of tribal peasants, the monarchy, and the priesthood. These are three durable and insistent forces at work in the shaping of Israel's tradition; for each of them much is at stake in the shaping of the tradition, and in the mapping of territory. Given these stunning differences, one may ask, "How is it possible that the same territory could be so differently and variously mapped?" The answer is that maps are not simply presentations of real estate. They are, rather, constructions of social reality that are informed by and grounded in different, often competing interests. The fact that maps are interested constructions of social reality gives mapmakers in every circumstance great freedom for articulating territory in many different ways. It follows, moreover, that no map is the "final" map, but every map may expect, soon or late, to be replaced by news maps that reflect new interests and new arrangements of social power. Because every map is a construction, every map is subject to deconstruction.

It may be noticed, in passing, that we do not have a mapping of pre-Israel Canaan. It may be that the list of conquered kings in Judges 12:7–24 is the offer of such a map. These several kings represent various city-states, some of which were larger and more powerful than others. The territory controlled by every city-state and every city-king would have been fluid, determined by how far its economic, cultural, and military force could reach. We do not have such a map, because Israel's constructionists would have had no interest in such territorial claims by the Canaanites because they uniformly regarded such claims as superseded by the promise of YHWH and by the occupation of Israel. It is plausible to think, as well, that as the borders of Canaanite city-states were fluid, so the boundaries of tribal Israel were also fluid. Mapmakers characteristically focus on a particular moment in time through which that instant of fluidity is rendered as a state of fixity. We should not, however, be fooled by such mapping, whether by the peasants, the kings or the priests. We are able to conclude that these various maps in their temporality are not unlike "our little systems that have their day and cease to be." For ancient Israel the larger empires north and south were dangerously at hand, awaiting an opportunity to redraw the map according to their imperial requirements.

Not surprisingly, what we see as mapmaking (and map unmaking) in ancient Israel is a process that has been replicated in the modern world. We may notice three moments in such mapmaking that readily confirms the ongoing process of mapmaking and map unmaking.

1. The "discovery" of America by Europeans in the service of Spain and the other great powers in the fifteenth and sixteenth centuries led to vigorous mapmaking for the New World. (As with the pre-Israelite Canaanites, we have no map of "prediscovery" America, though we have many tracings of the spheres of influence of various native tribal communities.) As with the Canaanite city-states, so tribal territories were surely fluid, depending on the reach of economic, cultural, and military effectiveness.

   It is not surprising that the "Age of Discovery" led promptly to the "Doctrine of Discovery." (That this period of exploration and colonialization is called "the Age of Discovery" makes it sound like no one [no one of importance!] lived in the land of the New World until the Europeans arrived.) The Doctrine of Discovery is a papal edict in 1493 (one year after Columbus in 1492!) that divided the New World between Spain and Portugal, and gave the European powers full control of and rights to the resources and populations of the New World. The occupation of the New World is a close parallel to the land promise and occupation of Israel that, as much as possible, disposed of the extant Canaanite population. The work of "discovery" and the papal edict both required and permitted new mappings of the New World, mappings that would variously assign territory to the several European powers. The mappings bespeak a new historical reality that could readily disregard many of the "facts on the ground" in the interest of the greedy European states. The new mappings were shameless assertions of European primacy as the great powers divided the land and its resources and populations among themselves. We are particularly familiar with the maps of the New World as we study, variously, the Louisiana Purchase, the dislocation of Spain from Florida, and the French and Indian Wars. All of these efforts to remap the New World were according to new arrangements of wealth and power. The maps helped to give an aura of legitimacy to the new claims.

2. After the final defeat of Napoleon, the Congress of Vienna in 1814–15 featured a new territorial settlement in Europe imposed by the Great Powers on devastated Europe. The purpose of the assembly in Vienna was to restore a peaceable international order, to assure the security and well-being of the ancient regimes, and to curb any further mischief by the force of France. Because the Great Powers were all present to the mapmaking, these powers were free to draw new territorial lines and so to make a new map of Europe. They of course paid great attention to traditional claims. But they also had freedom to recast power claims in a way that was supportive of Great Power interests.

3. Amid World War I, the British and French diplomats Mark Sykes and Francois Georges Picot arrived at a secret agreement to carve up the soon-to-be-defeated Ottoman Empire. This secret agreement was with the tacit consent of Russia and Italy. The two representatives quite freely and actively divided up the Ottoman Empire with an eager eye on the rich oil deposits in the Near East. Because the two representatives had behind them the major powers in the war, they had complete, arbitrary, and unrestrained freedom to draw new territorial lines for populations that were quite unrepresented in the secret negotiations that served only the interests of the two major powers. The result was the creation of artificial states in the Near East that paid no attention to traditional relationships.

When we consider in sequence the early maps of "discovery," the remapping of the Congress of Vienna, and the Sykes-Picot Agreement, we are able to see that the world, in its several parts, can be mapped and remapped according to active power interests. And while every mapmaker may imagine that the "new map" is the "final map," we are able to see that every new power configuration requires and permits new mapping that will readily displace and replace old mappings that were once thought to be final. This repeated remapping in the modern world is a fair replication of the remapping we have seen in the Old Testament, reflective of peasant, royal, and priestly interests. Thus every new map is one that can and will be deconstructed and reconstructed. There is and will be no final map.

I indicated at the outset that I have been led to this reflection on mapping and remapping by the remarkable study of Jo Guldi. In her final chapter (354–81), Guldi considers mapping as a strategy whereby landless people may come into possession of land. Guldi observes that paper is an instrument whereby control over territory is gained and maintained. To consider this mystifying power of paper, it has been possible among landless people to recognize that paper (cheap paper!)

can be "an instrument of popular power" (356–57). Guldi cites efforts at remapping in Appalachia and Ireland whereby landless peasants walk the land, observe with their eyes, and reduce what they see to paper in order to counter "official claims." Thus the maps drawn by the landless are a form of "participatory research" and a practice of self-governance (357):

> *The community walk of gathering data was itself a retooling of the appropriate technology version of the "transect survey," Alexander von Humboldt's technique of walking in a straight line up a mountain to identify ecological zones. By adapting Humboldt's method to the task of economic inquiry, researchers at Sussex retooled a technique of data collection for the purposes of community—rather than expert—knowledge. . . . The community walk was intended to excavate oral and tacit ways of knowing from sometimes illiterate communities. Inhabitants would discuss crops, soil, wells, and ownership in practical terms that arose from viewing each landscape, following their own intuitive categories rather than those imposed by the social scientist's agenda. Crediting nonelites and nonexperts with their own understanding removed indigenous, colonized, and working-class people from the category of "primitive" once assigned by Western colonizers and anthropologists—instead underscoring the practical, interpersonal, and moral intelligence implicit in any given culture. (360–61)*

This effort by the landless is done in knowing awareness that

> *the map was, after all, one of the foremost objects of empire, having been a tool of centralized administration and colonial rule since the origin of the cadastral map in sixteenth-century Europe. By the seventeenth century, European maps were*

> *helping settlers lay claim to the land of other peoples around the globe. By the nineteenth century, expert civil engineers and urban planners were using maps to evict poor families from neighborhoods known to house working-class radicals. . . .*
>
> *Of all of the groups of peasants that had lost their land through eviction, displacement, or indebtedness, the native tribes in North America had experienced the most extreme injustice. . . . As they began to look for a way to ask the Canadian government to enforce their property rights in order to exclude miners from their territory, they became aware of the power of maps; in government courts, the map was a tool to mandate adherence to property law. (365)*

Thus participatory mapping consists in the landless becoming active agents in the construction of their own future, along with a refusal to be passive recipients of the "paper" imposed on them by reigning power.

The accent of his new practice of mapping is on active participation:

> *Organizers had realized that even cheap material could be used in a process that stressed new habits of mind, suited to the inclusion of persons formerly excluded from the institutions of rule. (369)*

Special mention should be made of the singular work of John Gaventa. His early work was as a director of research at the Highlander Institute in Tennessee (371). More recently Gaventa is a lecturer at the University of Sussex, which is the most important center for work on participatory mapping, and thus land reform, with the recovery of land by landless peasants. The specific economic gains are to be matched by a recovery of consciousness concerning one's agency for one's future and the future of one's people.

When Ed and I did "map study" in Blackburn, we had no clue that a map was an instance of power and control. Given the threats of accumulated or absolute power and technological control, the summons to participation in remapping the world in human ways is an urgent imperative. One might begin in one's own neighborhood by mapping out power, control, and ownership, by observing how some possess and how the excluded might join in participation. We Bible believers belong to a long line of folk who have not hesitated to remap the world according to our best hopes.

Learning: when there is sufficient energy, will, and imagination, the present map of sociopolitical, economic power can be redrawn reconstructed. The "present sketch" is not a given!

Part VI

NEW HEAVEN

Our prophetic work in prayer is to entertain alternate worlds. Yes, to help God imagine God being a different, better kind of God. The prophetic imagination is performed in God's face as an act of risky courage. And progressives would never risk that because progressives do not think that prayer is a real transaction and therefore our prayers are mainly very innocuous. I think good prayer has to be more robust than that, meaning taking seriously that there's really somebody, on the other end, who is engaged in the process. I suppose the actual practice of my prayers is what I did at the beginning of class every day. I think my work in those prayers was to catch the students off balance. So I wanted my prayers not to be wholly predictable. And therefore, I thought, what are the ways in which you can use language that causes people to be a bit off balance and that invite God to be a bit off balance. I don't address God by name at the beginning of a prayer because I think we are always in the middle of a conversation. So you pick up the conversation at that moment.

Jeremiah dared to imagine that the abyss is what God called God's people into. What I appreciate is the way that what Jeremiah saw tore him up inside. It couldn't help but do that, and it was by being torn up inside that he arrived at these incredible utterances. I think his being torn up inside caused his imagination to move beyond all the categories that he could control. I think Jeremiah found himself either writing or saying things that he never intended to write or say but he was required to say them by where he found himself. That that may be the case of every serious artist, I don't know.

18

WHEN WATER DOES NOT WIN

LONG AGO WE had water in our basement. Seeking help, we happened on a wise old man who came to help us. He began with us didactically: "Water always wins." He meant that water is relentless; it cannot be controlled or eliminated. It can be channeled, but it will have a decisive say. In the end he nicely channeled the water away from our house and we had a dry basement.

These wise words, "Water always wins," came to my mind a few Sundays ago in church when one of our two favorite soloists, Dave, sang "Eternal Father Strong to Save:"*

Eternal father, strong to save,
Whose arm does bind the restless wave,
Who bids the mighty ocean deep
Its own appointed limits keep;
O hear us when we cry to Thee
For those in peril on the sea.

---

* A funny aside. Long ago I did an extended gig of teaching at Fourth Presbyterian Church in Chicago alongside my good friend, John Buchanan. Having ample free time there, one day I attended a funeral in the sanctuary of Fourth Church. The deceased, unknown to me, was a high-ranking naval officer, perhaps an admiral. At the end of the service as the casket was exiting, the organist played the postlude. It was supposed to be "Eternal Father strong to save," fitting for a naval officer. But the organist had failed to understand the assignment. Instead, what was played as "Anchors Away." I suspect that was the only time that song was played in the sanctuary at Fourth Church.

O Savior, whose almighty word
The winds and waves submissive heard,
Who walked upon the foaming deep,
And calm amid the rage did sleep;
O hear us when we cry to Thee
For those in peril on the sea.
O Holy Spirit, who did brood
Upon the waters dark and rude,
And bid their angry tumult cease,
And give for wild confusion peace;
O hear us when we cry to Thee
For those in peril on the sea.
O Trinity of love and pow'r,
Your children shield in danger's hour;
From rock and tempest, fire, and foe,
Protect them where-so- e'er they go;
Thus, ever more shall rise to Thee
Glad hymns of praise from land and sea.
"Eternal Father Strong to Save" (William Whiting)

By its particular use, this hymn is strongly linked to the US Navy. It conjures up images of mighty ships, with saluting officers and corps of sailors in line and at attention. But of course the hymn itself is not noticeably linked to the Navy. Rather it takes up the mighty surging waters of chaos, engages in prayer to the creator God, and petitions God's rescuing help for all those "in peril on the sea." The first stanza celebrates the capacity of the creator to limit the seas, to say to the surging waters, "Thus far and no farther" (see Jer 5:22). The second stanza alludes to the narrative of Jesus walking on the water (see John 6:16–21), and the third verse imagines the moment when the creator God tamed *tohu wabohu* (see Genesis 1:2). The final stanza is a more generic petition for God's protection from many threats, including wild tempest, fire, and foe. In all the hymn, in its grand solemnity, affirms the capacity of God to maintain a safely ordered creation amid coursing chaos. It is easy enough to link this recognition of chaos to the particular risks and dangers of those at sea, thus the risks and dangers of those in the Navy. The prayer is that they be kept safely. Indeed the hymn is a prayer that the waters—the seething forceful disorder of chaos—need not win.

In its prescientific articulation of creation, ancient Israel understood that the created order of the world is sustained by the creator God who held back the chaotic waters that were all around the earth, and that were endlessly moving against the created order in threatening ways. The safety and well-being of creation depends on the durable, constant attentiveness of the creator. But Israel could also bring this cosmic imagery down to cases, so that it knew about the real threat of real waters. Thus in Psalm 107, we get four exemplar instances of God's mighty rescuing power concerning those in the desert, those in prison, the sick, and those at sea. In the fourth stanza of the psalm, the doxology concerns those who "went down to the sea in ships":

Some went down to the sea in ships,
doing business on the mighty waters;
they saw the deeds of the LORD,
his wondrous works in the deep.
For he commanded and raised the stormy wind,
which lifted up the waves of the sea.
They mounted up to heaven, they went down to the depths;
their courage melted away in their calamity;
they reeled and staggered like drunkards,
and were at their wits' end.
Then they cried to the LORD in their trouble,
and he brought them out from their distress;
he made the storm be still,
and the waves of the sea were hushed.

Then they were glad because they had quiet,
and he brought them to their desired haven.
Let them thanks the Lord for his steadfast love,
for his wonderful works to humankind.
Let them extol him in the congregation of the people,
and praise him in the assembly of the elders. (Ps 107:23–32)

This narrative recital of human emergency and divine rescue follows the rhetorical pattern established in the previous verses. In each case the crisis is described. Second, those in emergency "cried out to the Lord," and were immediately heard. The rescue by God follows promptly upon the prayer of petition. The fourth element in each case is thanks to YHWH for YHWH's "steadfast love" that YHWH enacts through the rescue. In each case, including the fourth one on water, YHWH presides over the threat. Israel readily recognizes the decisive action of YHWH and sings praise. In the third case in verse 33, the act of thanks is reinforced by the offering of thanksgiving sacrifices (on which see Ps 116:12–19).

Thus our "naval hymn" echoes and reiterates a theme from Scripture that assures a worldview in which our "safe place" is kept safe by the capacity of the creator God to order, limit, and subdue the mighty forces of chaos. That capacity of the creator to manage chaos is, moreover, celebrated in the doxology of Psalm 29. The psalm describes a mighty storm, but then concludes with the dramatic affirmation that YHWH is "enthroned over the waters" (v. 10). That is, YHWH has made the waters so stable in their submissiveness to YHWH that God can use the chaotic waters for the base of the divine throne. God has not vanquished them, but they are fully subdued and robbed of their threatening power.

There is no doubt that the Gospel writers appeal to this tradition of God's governance of the chaotic waters in the narrative of Jesus stilling the storm (Mark 4:35–41; Matt 8:23–27; Luke 8:22–25).

In the narrative Mark 4:37 reports on the dangerous threat of the waters:

> *A great windstorm arose, and the waves beat into the boat, so that the boat was already being swamped.*

The disciples at sea with Jesus are terrified; they know what the storm can do; that is, they know that chaos can undo their ordered world. They have no recourse except to Jesus whom they awaken. They awaken him, for he is their only chance for safety. Jesus is at his lordly best. He simply utters a royal command to the waters:

> *Peace, be still. (v. 39)*

That is all; the wind stops, the waves are subdued. He offers no explanation. But he leaves his disciples in wonderment:

> *Who is this, that even the wind and the sea obey him? (v. 41)*

They know the answer to their question. The answer is old and established in Israel. The one who governs the waters is the creator God. In this narrative no dots are explicitly connected. But the point is mistakable. This Jesus in the boat with them is none other than the creator God who also governs the waters. Israel had long affirmed that their God "neither slumbers nor sleeps" (Ps 121:4). But Jesus goes one better. He sleeps! He sleeps, perhaps because he is human. Or he sleeps because he has complete confidence in his mastery of chaos. Either way, the frightened disciples are made safe and secure from all alarms. Israel has always found its well-being in the goodness of God, and now that governance has become specific for them. The claim is further escalated in John 6:16–21, wherein Jesus walks on water, a majestic act echoed in the third verse of the "naval hymn," thus patrolling his domain.

Dave's solo, the wise words of our "water man," Israel's tradition of doxology, and the lordly power of Jesus were, altogether, on my mind as I recalled the frequent, almost daily reports of migrants who travel by boat at great risk at sea in their transport to a better land. They are often destroyed in the process of transport. Thus as I write this here is a headline for the day:

> *"Dozens of Migrants Die after Boat Sinks in Strait of Sicily"* (New York Times, *August 9, 2023*).

It could have been any day or nearly every day. The migrants are victims of "unscrupulous smugglers" who put them at risk with dysfunctional boats. But they are also victims of the violent lands from which they flee, and victims of the lands to which they come what are characteristically unwelcoming and inhospitable. For example, Garret Hardin in "The Tragedy of the Commons," *Science* 162 (1968) famously warned that the "bottom of the barrel" migrants will, if unchecked, overwhelm the luxurious "commons" of the US. The migrants might easily conclude that "water always wins." With the image of these migrants in boats at risk, I listened again to Dave's solo. What if those "at peril on the sea" are not naval officers, but migrants who are ill-clad, unidentified, and without resources? Thus the naval hymn might be their prayer as well.

With the migrants in boats front and center, we might ponder again the verdict, "Water always wins"! The migrants, in their risky venture, might reach this conclusion drawn by our old water man. The cadences of faith suggest, alternatively, that water does not and cannot win when the "Eternal Father" is strong to save. But then we may tease out the quotidian reality of that faith claim:

> *Water does not win when the faithful people of God take steps to protect these migrants.*
>
> *Water does not win if host governments become more receptive of refugees.*

> *Water does not win if we come to regard migrants traveling in boats not as an unwelcome intrusion, but rather as neighbors in desperate need.*
>
> *Water does not win if we take seriously our generic mandate to protect the defenseless from the ruthless power of chaos and extend it especially to these people.*

We may take these several allusions to water as an articulation of the reality of surging chaos. When we do that, we may recognize that ours is a time of great displacement of many peoples. The reality of climate change causes many people, of necessity, to flee to higher ground. The current brutality of war and the menace of a predatory economics require people to find safety elsewhere. Consequently our time is inescapably a time of great movement of large numbers of vulnerable people who by their very existence are committed to find safe places to live. It is high time to recognize that, for all of the church's preoccupation with individual "sin," the reality of our time is one of chaos that is partly the product of the human enterprise, but partly the work of untamed evil among us.

When we human beings accept our proper role as managers of creation, then our work is to be alert to the threat of chaos, regardless of its cause, and to create conditions for orderly, viable well-being. Dave's solo appeals to the creator God on behalf of all those "in peril on the sea." Along with such a petition to the Eternal Father, of course, the work is to contribute to the possibility of a viable social order and the practice of social justice for all parties.

The Bible is eventually an act of hope. Among the most extreme hopes voiced in the Bible is the vision of a new heaven, a new earth, and a new Jerusalem. And then this:

> *The sea is no more. (Rev 21:1)*

The expectation is breathtaking. The faith of Israel and of the church is the capacity to imagine a world where chaos is no more. Chaos will be overcome by the decree of the creator God, and by the tenacious, sustained work of the human community in its solidarity with all the creatures who depend on a well-ordered creation.

19

THE END OF IMAGINATION?

MOST OF WHAT I know about imagination I have learned from the varied dense writings of Paul Ricoeur. I have concluded that imagination is the capacity to host a world other than the one that is in front of us. Such an act of hosting an alternative world is inherently subversive, as it serves to question and override the world in front of us that we too easily take as given. From this it follows that those who have an inordinate stake in the world immediately in front of us—whether that stake is socioeconomic, political, moral, theological—will do what they can to discourage or prevent imagination in order that we may settle into the present world as an immutable given.

In my book *The Prophetic Imagination*, and many times thereafter, I have explored the way in which the prophets (and the prophetic books) of the Old Testament are master examples of the practice of imagination that regularly served to deabsolutize and deconstruct the world of royal priestly ambition in ancient Israel. They did so, moreover, in the face of royal ideology and temple liturgies that sought to establish that world as an immutable, God-given wonder, a gift of God's goodness. In that ancient world prophetic imagination saw that the royal-priestly world of Jerusalem was *a construct* that willfully stacked the cards of political, economic power in greedy ways, and so had to be *deconstructed* for the sake of an alternative future in Israel. This remarkable cluster of prophetic texts that practice such imagination are presented under the rubric of "Thus saith the Lord," or "The word of the Lord came to me." Such formulae credit such imaginative utterance to the authority of God, thus issuing in "divine oracles." That rubric, however, has caused us not to notice, as boldly as we might, that these utterances are fresh, daring human utterances that practice subversion against the *status quo* that had been made to appear immutable and "safe and secure from all alarms." This surge of prophetic imagination in that covenantal corpus revolves, in turn, around two reference points. First, *speeches of judgment* against Israel that yield sanctions of exile or destruction that are said to be YHWH's own work. And second, great *anticipations of newness* that God will work as an act of fidelity that will override all historical circumstance. In both cases of *judgment* and *promise*, the prophets assert that the world in front of Israel cannot fend off the coming work of God. That is, Israel's prosperity and security *cannot fend off divine judgments* of exile and destruction. Conversely, Israel's alienation and despair *cannot fend off the resolve of YHWH* to make of Israel a "new thing" in the world. Such imagination refuses to accept present historical reality as a "given." Rather, it sees such present circumstance as a social construction that can be deconstructed, and by the power of God construed alternatively. This prophetic imagination bears witness to the sovereignty of God that is not defined by or contained in present social reality.

In the midst of Israel's peace and prosperity the prophets can imagine a world of YHWH's governance wherein *Israel stands under acute divine sanction* for its violation of Torah. Thus prophetic imagination is counterintuitive, based in a conviction of YHWH's uncompromising rule, even in the face of Israel's peace and prosperity.

- In the midst of Israel's prosperity, Amos can readily voice a sad lament, because Israel has a future coming from YHWH that it does not yet anticipate:

Hear this word that I take up over you in lamentation,
O house of Israel:

Fallen, no more to rise,
is maiden Israel;

forsaken on her land,
with none to raise her up. (Amos 5:1–2)

- By a wordplay Amos can imagine the "end" while Israel itself relies on its continuing prosperity:

"The end has come upon my people Israel;
I will never again pass them by.
The songs of the temple shall become wailing in that day,"
says the Lord GOD;
"the dead bodies shall be many,
cast out in every place. Be silent!" (Amos 8:2–3)

- Micah addresses the predatory forces in Israel that covet and seize the property of others who are vulnerable. He can anticipate a time to come when the successful land speculators will say, with bitter lamentation:

We are utterly ruined;
the LORD alters the inheritance of my people;
how he removes it from me!
Among our captors he parcels out our fields. (Mic 2:4)

Micah imagines that the land will be redistributed and the aggressive speculators will have no share in the new distribution (Mic 2:5).

- Isaiah can mock the wealthy women of Jerusalem who love to strut in public. He foresees a time when their wealth strut will be reduced to the shame-filled status of slaves:

The LORD will afflict with scabs
the heads of the daughters of Zion,
and the LORD will lay bear their secret parts. (Isa 3:17)

In the inventory of finery that follows in Isaiah 3:18–23, we may imagine the prophet having some pernicious delight in fingering the clothes closets of the women, as he probes décor, item by item. This inventory, moreover, is followed in 3:24 with a fivefold "instead" in which the prophet traces out the socioeconomic demise and shame of the rich and successful women who had thought they had no accountability to anyone for anything. The ultimacy of YHWH's rule evokes radical reversals in the lives of those who mock that rule.

- Perhaps the ultimate prophetic articulation of such divine judgment is offered by Jeremiah who can imagine, point by point, the undoing of all creation:

I looked on the earth, and lo, it was waste and void;
and to the heavens, and they had no light.
I looked on the mountains, and lo, they were quaking,
and all the hills moved to and fro.
I looked, and lo, there was no one at all,
and all the birds of the air had fled.
I looked, and lo, the fruitful land was a desert,
and all its cities were laid in ruins
before the LORD, before his fierce anger. (Jer 4:23–26)

The sum of these prophetic utterances of judgment is to place before Israel a world other than the one that is in front of them. The world in front of them was all comfort, success, security, and prosperity. The other world of prophetic imagination, to the contrary, is one of *loss, shame, and suffering*. The intent of such poetry is to deabsolutize the present world that could all too easily be taken as an assured circumstance, guaranteed by an attentive God whose commitment to Israel is taken to be perpetual and unconditional.

The matter is the same in the utterances of prophetic hope that imagines that God will generate for Israel a future that is counter to the present world of loss, displacement, misery, and death. It was easy enough for Israel, in the ruthless hands of the Assyrian and Babylonian armies, to fall into despair and resignation. The miserable facts on the ground could have dictated exactly such a mood of helplessness and hopelessness in Israel. The prophets, however, insist otherwise. They insist otherwise because the future yet to come will not be determined by either imperial power or by Israel's despair, but by the deep resolve and intent of God who is now said to be utterly faithful. Israel comes to regard its loss, defeat, and displacement as a sign of God's abandonment. In the anticipation of the prophets, however, such a negative circumstance is penultimate, because the faithful God wills well-being for Israel.

- Thus in agrarian imagery, Amos can anticipate the renewal of the productivity of agriculture with inexplicable abundance:

The time is surely coming, says the L*ORD*,
when the one who plows shall overtake the one who reaps,
and the treader of grapes the one who sows the seed;
the mountains shall drip sweet wine,
and all the hills shall flow with it. (Amos 9:13)

- In a remarkably cunning oracular utterance Hosea can perform the history of Israel according to the imagery of an angry separation and a failed divorce (Hos 2:2–13). This powerful relational imagery, in turn, makes it possible for the prophet to imagine a re-wooing of Israel by YHWH, and a subsequent remarriage in utter fidelity (vv. 4–20). In the newly recited wedding vows, voiced by husband-YHWH, the prophet can reiterate all of the great covenantal vocabulary of fidelity on God's part:

I will take you for my wife in righteousness and in justice, in steadfast love, and in mercy. I will take you for my wife in faithfulness, and you shall know the L*ORD*. *(Hos 2:19–20)*

- Best known among such promissory oracles is the anticipation of Isaiah 2:2–4 and Micah 4:1–4. According to this expectation, a new day is coming on God's people. It will be a day when the generous rule of YHWH is fully established. That generous rule will make Jerusalem and its temple the epicenter of international well-being, as other nations are eager to be instructed in Israel's Torah. The practical result of such international study of Torah is that there will be general disarmament:

> *They shall beat their swords into plowshares,*
> *and their spears into pruning hooks;*
> *nation shall not lift up sword against nation,*
> *neither shall they learn war any more. (Isa 2:4)*

Micah adds to the oracle a caveat that the outcome of such disarmament will be the flourishing of a peasant economy that is not extravagant or overly ambitious or indulgent:

> *But they shall sit under their own vines and under their own fig trees,*
> *and no one shall make them afraid;*
> *for the mouth of the* Lord *of hosts has spoken. (Mic 4:4)*

- And even hard-nosed Ezekiel, in his singularly begrudging way, can anticipate that YHWH will gather the scattered people of Israel and bring them home to Jerusalem (Ezek 36:24). The people shall be made "clean," that is, fit for the worship of YHWH (36:25), and they shall enjoy agricultural abundance with no shortage of food:

> *I will summon the grain and make it abundant and lay no famine upon you. I will make the fruit of the tree and the produce of the field abundant, so that you may never*

again suffer the disgrace of famine among the nations. (Ezek 36:29–30)

All of these prophetic promises (and many more) are grounded in the conviction that God governs the creation, and that YHWH will enact YHWH's will for Israel and for all creation, even in the face of desperate circumstances to the contrary.

- The ultimate prophetic anticipation in the Old Testament is Isaiah 65:17–25, which awaits a new heaven, a new earth, and a new Jerusalem, all of which are unlike the old world already known in Israel:

For I am about to create new heavens
and a new earth;
the former things shall not be remembered
or come to mind.
But be glad and rejoice forever
in what I am creating,
for I am about to create Jerusalem as a joy
and its people as a delight . . .
they shall not hurt or destroy
on all my holy mountain,
says the Lord. (Isa 65:17–18, 25)

Here as elsewhere, the prophet does not explain. This is not prediction. It is poetry. It is the lining out of an alternative scenario that invites Israel to a new prospect of hope that has within it a new undertaking of on-the-ground practical obedience.

Thus in both *speeches of judgment* and *promises of hope*, the prophets, taken in sum and taken utterance by utterance, invite Israel not to hold too closely the world in front of it. That is, do not hold too closely *a world of well-being*, because it is fragile and will not be sustained. Do not absolutize it. Or alternatively, do not hold too closely *a world of despair*, as though it were a fate to perpetuity. Do not hold too closely either *a world of prosperity* or a *world of hopelessness*. Because this and every such world is penultimate to the will and purpose of YHWH. Thus the prophetic utterances claim to be in sync with the holy God who is beyond our capture or domestication. Israel is summoned to live with the freedom of penultimacy, with new futures yet to emerge from the sovereignty of God.

I had all of this in mind as I read a book, *The End of Imagination* by Arundhati Roy, (Haymarket, 2016). Roy is a bold Indian writer, an active advocate for justice, and recipient of the Booker Prize in 1997. Her book has a suggestive appearance, as the term "Imagination," on both the front cover and on the binding, is crossed out by what looks like purple ink. The book is a collection of her "woke" essays over time. The titular article, "The End of Imagination" (45–64), concerns the development—in India and Pakistan—of the capacity for an atomic bomb. She writes of that moment in 1998 when the bomb became a possibility in these two juxtaposed countries:

> *If only, if* only, *nuclear war was just another kind of war. If only it was about the usual things—nations and territories, gods and histories. If only those of us who dread it are just worthless cowards who are not prepared to die in defense of our beliefs. If only nuclear war was the kind of war in which countries battle countries and men battle men. But it isn't. If there is a nuclear war, our foes will not be China or America or even each other. Our foe will be the earth itself. The very elements—the sky, the air, the land, the wind and water—will turn against us. Their wrath will be terrible.*
>
> *Our cities and forests, our fields and villages will burn for days. Rivers will turn to poison. The air will become fire. The wind will spread the flames. When everything there is to burn has been burned and the fires die, smoke will rise and shut out the sun. The earth will be enveloped in darkness.*

> *There will be no day. Only interminable night. Temperatures will drop to far below freezing and nuclear winter will set in. Water will turn into toxic ice. Radioactive fallout will seep through the earth and contaminate ground water. Most living things, animal and vegetable, fish and fowl, will die. Only rats and cockroaches will breed and multiply and compete for what little food there is. (46–47)*

Roy understands this moment in her writing as the moment when imagination almost came to an end, when we could no longer think of anything to write or to say, because the bomb had precluded all work of imagination. She is able to imagine the threat and fear so massive and compelling that it brings to an end the enterprise of human freedom and human possibility. In subsequent essays Roy unfolds the emergency her country faces because of Prime Minister Modi and his Bharatiya Janata Party, which is increasingly framed as an extreme form of Hindu nationalism that amounts to a deep fascist threat to non-Hindus in their natural country.

By way of analogue I suppose that the development of the bomb by these two national communities has as impact not unlike the deportation from Northern Israel in 722 BCE (2 Kings 17:5–6) and from Judah in 587 BCE (Jer 52:24–30). Thus history "stopped"; imagination ceased! As did the reportage of these writings. One could not imagine, for a time, a future out beyond such an event of deep dislocation. That is the "end of imagination" of which Roy writes. But of course she herself, to the contrary, has not ceased to imagine. She has continued, not unlike the ancient prophets, to imagine out beyond the deathly limits of the moment to a future that is beyond human expectation.

Like Roy, we in the US live in a society that is prone to eliminate imagination because it is inherently subversive of the status quo. While we may have moved, for now, beyond the numbing imposed by the threat of nuclear war (even while it remains real enough!), other factors militate against imagination. Most especially, it is the force of the ideology of capitalism that makes it difficult to imagine a world out beyond present economic reality. Note well: I have not said "capitalism," but rather the "ideology of capitalism" that has become the measure and regulator of all social reality among us. The capacity to imagine outside the limits of that ideology is a tall mandate, one that must be faced and embraced.

Thus in the face of any would-be "end of imagination," it remains the work of those of us in the church to foster and support the arts (as instruments for imagination), and to be engaged in imagination that lines out a world where the rule of the Crucified One is operative. It is important to recognize that the chief work of the church is artistic, namely, to offer, trust in, and act toward a world other than the one that is in front of us. The world in front of us has largely succumbed to false ideology. But grounding in the reality of the cross (where truth meets pain) offers an opening for an alternative world.

It is important for congregations and pastors to remember that we are primarily in the *imagination business*. It is our work to line out what the world is like as Christ presides over it. The best and most readily available material we have for such imagination is the collage of the parables of Jesus that tell of a world other than the one that is in front of us. This is the world of a man who had two sons, a world occupied by the Good Samaritan, a world of final judgment for sheep and goats, and a final banquet for all. This is a world in which matters unfold amid surprise, gift, and abundance. It is the work of Christian liturgy to line out that world with freedom and playfulness. It follows that the church defaults on its mandate to imagine when it settles for didacticism, or to put it colloquially, "man-splaining." The imaginative work of the church intends to break open the world of fear, to witness to "a more excellent way" beyond scorekeeping and vengeance, and to show that we may alternatively practice a world of hospitality, generosity, forgiveness, and abundance. It was of course this practice of Jesus toward the socially rejected that finally made him a threat against the status quo that required his elimination. That, nevertheless, is the work entrusted to us. And when we become didactic and explanatory, we fail.

The practice of imagination, in our lifetime, has come to a wondrously dramatic moment in the "Dream Speech" of Martin Luther King. In that utterance King took on the role of prophetic imagination and invited us to a world other than the world of bigotry and exclusion all around us. And he was assassinated because such dream constitutes an undoing of the status quo. Thus for every dreamer of such a dangerous dream, there are *The Killers of the Dream*, as Lillian Smith has poignantly shown (Norton, 1949). It is no wonder that the established powers in ancient Israel had to kill the prophets:

> *Now Obadiah revered the LORD greatly; when Jezebel was killing off the prophets of the Lord, Obadiah took a hundred prophets, hid them fifty to a cave, and provided them with bread and water. (1 Kings 18:3–4; see 18:13; Lam 2:20)*

And it is no wonder that Jesus grieved over Jerusalem that kills the prophets, even as he understood about his own risk in the city:

> *Woe to you! For you build tombs for the prophets whom your ancestors killed. (Luke 11:47)*
>
> *Jerusalem, Jerusalem, the city that kills the prophets and stones those who are sent to it! (Luke 13:33; see Matthew 23:29–31)*

This imagination for which the prophets were killed is our proper work. Our future depends on it. In the face of the "end of imagination" in her society, Roy can write,

> *We're radioactive already, and the war hasn't even begun. So stand up and say something. Never mind that it's been*

> *said before. Speak up on your own behalf. Take it very personally.* (50)

So say we all. The fight is conducted by imagery, poetry, arts of all kinds including the playful utterance of the gospel that refuses the domestication of the Israelite kings, the Roman governors, or the pressures of capitalism. The truth comes as artful subversion. Our lives and our world depend on it. It is only such a *sub-version* of reality that will save us from the lethal force of the *dominant version.*

20

WRITTEN UP, WRITTEN DOWN

I CAN RECALL quite vividly two times in my teen years when I "signed up." First, at age thirteen I was confirmed by my father-pastor at St. Paul's E. and R. Church in Blackburn, Missouri. It was quite an event in the church. On the previous Sunday my confirmation mate, Vivian Kirchoff, and I were examined by my father on the catechism before the entire congregation. The Sunday after confirmation we joined in holy communion for the first time. On the Sunday of confirmation we processed into church. After the service Mr. Chester Grube, the church secretary, took Vivian and me to the back of the church where we signed the big book of church members. Mr. Grube made quite a dramatic event of the signing. In that moment we became full adult members of the church. All of this after we had reiterated the vow of the catechism:

Lord Jesus, for thee I live,

for thee I suffer,
for thee I die!

Lord Jesus, thine will I be in life and in death!
Grant me, O Lord, eternal salvation! Amen.

The second "signing up" was that at eighteen I went to Marshall, the county seat of our Saline County, with my dad and "registered" for the draft as was required by law. I had had extended conversation with my dad about the registration. I asked for and promptly received classification as IVD, a deferment for ministerial study. I had decided in my junior year in high school where I was headed. I had no sense at the time of the moral ambiguity of the classification. I was glad to be properly registered. In college I joined a throng of pretheological students who also had IVD classifications. These two "signings" situated me, as I finished high school, registered as church member and registered as a citizen.

All of this memory came back to me as I was astonished, yet again, to notice that in the early verses of Luke's birth narrative that the term *register* occurs four times:

> *A decree went out from Emperor Augustus that all the world should be registered. (2:1)*
> *This was the first registration and was taken while Quirinius was governor of Syria. (v. 2)*
> *All went to their own towns to be registered. (v. 3)*
> *He [Joseph] went to be registered with Mary. (v. 5)*

The narrative is framed as an imperial act of registration. The Greek term is *apographo*, that is, "written down." All were to be written down under imperial auspices in the same way I had been written down by the church and by the government. Joseph and Mary, vulnerable peasants from the shabby village of Nazareth, were written down by the empire in its long reach into the peasant economy. And of course, the only two conventional reasons for such imperial registration are to keep proper tax records for future taxation, and proper manpower rosters for future military drafts. Joseph exhibited no resistance against the registration. He engaged in no civil disobedience but complied with the imperial requirement.

That report concerning Caesar's registration is only an introduction for Luke. The real narrative, beginning in verse 8, is quite otherwise. The real narrative is about angelic messengers announcing the arrival of a savior, the Messiah, the Lord (v. 11). The messengers bespeak the emergence of an alternative governance. The shepherds, lowest of the lowly, likely even "lower" than Joseph the carpenter, were awed and moved to doxology that pushed outside of imperial boundaries. I wonder if the shepherds had "registered" with the empire of Rome. I wonder if they were "written down" by the empire. Perhaps they were too obscure and elusive to be caught in such a registration. We do not know; we only know that they were readily welcomed into an alternative governance. They gladly received it!

So I have wondered about being "written down." Joseph was written down! That is why he went from Nazareth to Bethlehem, in order to be written down. Maybe he would be recruited for imperial war. Almost certainly he would be taxed. But he and Mary did not flee to Egypt in order to avoid either the draft or taxation. They fled because they knew that that the local authority, a Jewish king, wanted their baby dead. They were written down by Rome, but they fled in fear for their lives. Being written down by the empire would never keep them safe!

It is enough to see, in Luke's framing of the birth narrative, that it was the empire's urge to get the family of the carpenter written down that created the venue for the messianic birth. This led me to consider other such acts of governmental "writing down" in Scripture.

The most dramatic case of such writing down is that of King David in 2 Samuel 24:1–9. Curiously, the census proposed by David was instigated through divine cunning (v. 1). From the outset we are put on notice that the census (writing down!) is inimical to the will of YHWH, who "incited" David in anger. David ordered the census (v. 2), but is immediately challenged by his leading general, Joab (v. 3). We know that Joab is an advocate of the old tribal order, so that later on he will oppose and resist the royal ambition of his son, Solomon (1 Kings 1:25; 2:28–35). Joab knowingly regards the proposed census as an excessive reach of royal power and a violation of old tribal protocol. Thus Joab's question to David is a tacit rebuke of the king. The king, however, does not even bother to respond to Joab. He proceeds promptly to the census, which is to be conducted by his military. If we consider the mode of implementation plus the summary statement of verse 9, we can see that the purpose of the census is the mobilization of military manpower:

> *Joab reported to the king the number of those who had been recorded: in Israel there were eight hundred thousand soldiers able to draw the sword, and those of Judah were five hundred thousand. (2 Sam 24:9)*

The census-taking military surveyed the entire land, down to every territory and village (vv. 5–8). They sought out every possible military recruit, a sum that was in the end quite impressive. The king could be reassured that he had ample manpower available for his military ambitions and adventures (see 2 Sam 8:1–14).

We are told at the outset of our narrative that YHWH "incited" (v. 1) David. It was as if YHWH jeopardized David by putting the idea in his head. The matter is made acutely ironic in verse 10. It finally occurred, even to David, that instigating the census was sinful. That judgment attributed to David here (and apparently to YHWH as well) reflects the old tribal resistance to royal regimentation, on which see 1 Samuel 8:11–13, which anticipates exactly such royal recruitment:

> *He [the king] will take your sons and appoint them to his chariots and to be his horsemen, and to run before his chariots; and he will appoint for himself commanders of thousands and commanders of fifties, and some to plow his ground and reap his harvest, and some to make his implements of war and the equipment of his chariots. He will take your daughters to be perfumers and cooks and bakers. (1 Sam 8:11–13)*

Thus the census is understood to be a part of the persistent predatory propensity of royal power in which David now participates. The acknowledgement of David (and of YHWH!) in 2 Samuel 24:10 is congruent with the objection raised by Joab earlier in the narrative. While YHWH does not directly condemn the census as sinful, the three options offered to David in 24:12–13 confirm the point. The census, whether by David or belatedly by Caesar, is a contradiction of YHWH's intent for social ordering. It is a sin for some with power to mobilize the clout over more vulnerable folk in order to implement their eagerness for domination and control.

The matter is tilted somewhat differently in the alternative version of the narrative in 1 Chronicles 21:1–6. In this rendering, the first verse has "Satan" incite David to initiate the census. As given here, Satan is no longer the "tester" of the Job narrative but is an instigator of evil. Thus the work of evoking evil by David is now separated from YHWH, who can be "displeased" by the census without being its instigator at the same time. Because Satan is now engaged, YHWH's own part in the narrative is much less ambiguous.

The only other scriptural mention of a census is voiced by Gamaliel, a "teacher of the law," in Acts 5:37. Gamaliel issues a cautionary word to his colleagues by citing an earlier case of such action. Almost incidentally he alludes to "Judas the Galilean" who resisted the imperial census:

> *After him Judas the Galilean rose up at the time of the census and got people to follow him; he also perished, and all who followed him were scattered. (Acts 5:37)*

His resistance to the census ended in death and disorder. Gamaliel has no good word to speak for the census, but warns against rash resistance to it. (This same census, according to Arndt and Gingrich, is also mentioned by Josephus, so it was a well-known event in the life of the community.) We are able to see the inclination of seriously religious people to resist royal regimentation via the census. It is not a good or wise matter to be "written down" by the regime. Such a writing down can only function to further the dangerous accumulation of power.

There is, however, an alternative writing down that is to be celebrated by the faithful. The matter is noted in three very different kinds of texts in the New Testament. First, when Jesus welcomes back the seventy from their successful restorative work, he warns that they should not rejoice in the success of their work. Rather, he says to the seventy faithful disciples,

> *Do not rejoice at this, that the spirits submit to you, but rejoice that your names are written in heaven. (Luke 10:20)*

The verb is the same as that used in the birth narrative (*apographo*). The imagery is of a scroll that contains the names of all those who are welcomed into the rule of God. This usage likely reflects the fact that Luke was a learned man who lived in a world of writing. Thus he can readily utilize imagery of a written roster of the faithful. Those who live out the restorative power of Jesus have their names written in the registry of the welcomed. We may imagine, though it is not stated, that the seventy were not registered with the empire, as they had a different "membership." They belonged elsewhere.

Second, the letter to the Hebrews bids the faithful under duress to fresh resolve for fidelity:

> *Therefore lift your drooping hands and strengthen your weak knees, and make straight paths for your feet, so that what is lame may not be put out of joint, but rather be healed. (Heb 12:12–13)*

And then the writer offers a sweeping assurance to the faithful:

> *But you have come to Mount Zion and to the city of the living God, the heavenly Jerusalem, and to innumerable*

> *angels in festal gathering, and to the assembly of the firstborn who are enrolled in heaven, and to God the judge of all, and to the spirits of the righteous made perfect, and to Jesus, the mediator of a new covenant, and to the sprinkled blood that speaks a better word than the blood of Abel. (vv. 22–24)*

In a flood of images, the faithful will have arrived at

> Mount Zion,
> the city of the living God,
> the heavenly Jerusalem,
> the assembly of the firstborn,
> God the judge of all,
> the spirits of the righteous, and
> to Jesus, the mediator of a new covenant.

The images pile up as a torrent. Our interest is in the phrase "the assembly of the firstborn who are enrolled" in heaven (v. 23). Again it is the verb *apographo*, "written down." Those who endure persecution in faithfulness will be admitted to the company of those who are written down in heaven, that is, in the realm where God, and not Caesar, presides.

Third, in the vision of the apocalypse, the "books were opened" (Rev 20:12). One of the books is "the book of life." In this vision, we have a tight quid pro quo, as tight as the rigor of the covenant of Deuteronomy. Records are kept of the way lives are lived, and all are judged "according to what they have done." Some were written in the book of life. But there is warning to those who do not get entry into the book of life:

> *Anyone whose name was not found written in the book of life was thrown into the lake of fire. (Rev 20:15)*

A different future "in heaven" is on offer for those who have lived faithfully and obediently. It is to these faithful, to them alone, that a wondrous future is on offer:

> *See, the home of God is among mortals.*
> *He will dwell with them;*
> *they will be his peoples,*
> *and God himself will be with them;*
> *he will wipe every tear from their eyes.*
> *Death will be no more;*
> *mourning and crying and pain will be no more,*
> *for the first things have passed away. (Rev 21:3–4)*

The ones excluded from this glorious future are left on the outside:

> *But as for the cowardly, the faithless, the polluted, the murderers, the fornicators, the sorcerers, the idolaters, and all liars, their place will be in the lake that burns with fire and sulfur, which is the second death. (v. 8)*

It is worth noting that the verb "written" is utilized to confirm the promise:

> *"See, I am making all things new." Also he said, "Write this, for these words are trustworthy and true." (v. 5)*

The substance of the promise to the faithful consists in "the water of life" (v. 6; see John 4:13–15), and a reiteration of the ancient covenantal formula:

> *I will be their God and they will be my children (v. 7).*

Thus the imagery of writing:

written in heaven (Luke 10:20)
written in heaven (Heb 12:23)
written in the book of life (Rev 20:15).

The verb is used in these three very different genres of literature; all offer an "enrollment" that is alternative to being "registered" by Caesar. All three usages appeal to the verb *apographo*, an invitation to a radical choice. One can be "written down" in either book, but not in both. Back in my teens, as I registered as a church member, and as I registered as a citizen, I had not seen the contradiction of these two registrations. Belatedly, in our current sociopolitical environment of violence, the either/or of these alternative "writings down" is much clearer to me and more generally. The community of the faithful might indeed be on notice about being "written down" or being "written up."

Footnote from my remembered reading:

> *Joad reports to Muley that he is out of prison on parole and has "Got to report ever so often." Muley asks Joad how it was in prison at McAlester. He responds:*
>
> *. . . I got along O.K. Minded my own business, like any guy would. I learned to write nice as hell. Birds an' stuff like that, too; not just word writin'. My ol' man'll be sore when he sees me whip out a bird in one stroke. Pa's gonna be mad when he sees me do that. He don't like no fancy stuff like that. He don't even like word writin'. Kinda scares 'im, I guess. Ever' time Pa seen writin', somebody took somepin away from 'im. (John Steinbeck,* The Grapes of Wrath *[Penguin, 1939], 69–70)*

Writing is an instrument of power; it mostly belongs to the regime that may "write up" one all the way from traffic tickets to income tax payments. The faithful are otherwise "written down." That is what happened when I was "confirmed," a matter of much more weight than either Mr. Grube or I understood at the time.

21

UNSHAKEABLE SYSTEMS

ON A RECENT Sunday morning before church, I looked at the notes strewn across my desk. Among them was this sentence by China Mieville, *A Spectre History: On the Communist Manifesto* (Haymarket, 2022), 73:

> *The Manifesto is clear that history is a long sequence of the upending and overturning of seemingly unshakeable systems.*

In the next sentences Mieville applies this observation of Marx and Engel to capitalism:

> *Capitalism may be inevitable. But we have no grounds for claiming this a priori.*

That is, in this judgment not even capitalism can be taken as "unshakeable. That left me a lot to think about while at church. In church we do not claim that "history" is the active agent in "overturning and upending." Rather we say it is the Lord of history, the one we confess in Jesus of Nazareth, who in cunning, hidden, and resolved ways does the overturning amid history.

> *The LORD of hosts has sworn,*
> *As I have designed,*
> *so shall it be;*
> *and as I have planned,*
> *so it shall come to pass . . .*

For the L*ORD of hosts has planned,*
and who will annul it?
His hand is stretched out,
and who will turn it back? (Isa 14:24, 27)

It is at this point that Christian faith goes beyond Marxian analysis. As I reflected on this claim by the church, I had the following three awarenesses press on me.

1. The church is a custodian for "unshakeable" claims, that is, claims, not systems. Thus the two great ecumenical creeds of the church lay down the "unshakeable" trinitarian claims of catholic faith. Or more concisely, it is the eucharistic formulation that articulates the bottom-line certitude of gospel faith:

Christ has died,
Christ is risen,
Christ will come again.

This is not to say that these claims are uncontested in the church. The claim that "Christ is risen" causes squirming interpretation in much of the liberal church. And that he is "coming again" is a great embarrassment, as such apocalyptic anticipation is alien to much establishment church faith in its "realized eschatology." Given these stark reservations, it is nonetheless clear that in some form, through some interpretation, these claims are elementally nonnegotiable for serious faith. One cannot finally imagine the historic church moving through time in some continuous way without these several claims. We may (and do!) mumble or minimize, but they are the sine qua non for our faith.

But a second matter struck me.

2. The church, through time, has been custodian for unshakeable claims that elementally betray the thick mystery of the gospel.

Thus the church has been and continues to be an eager custodian for patriarchy and has all too readily insisted on male authority and male domination (carried in patriarchal rhetoric and imagery) as essential to the church. In like manner the church in our society has been a willing co-conspirator in sustaining the ideology of white supremacy, so that some of the unshakeable claims of the church are simply uncritical appropriations from our distorted culture. And now, belatedly, we are able to see how much of the church continues to be custodian for unshakeable heterosexual hegemony, with only modest and grudging recognition now to the contrary. And if we may add to this roster of shame, the church willingly embraces nationalism so that in times of war the church readily signs on with the national effort in uncritical unthinking ways.

Beyond these unshakeable claims that contradict the gospel, we can see that when church faith is tilted to an extremity, we get distorted claims. Thus may lead, on the one hand, radical divine sovereignty, overstated to the extreme, means that human freedom will disappear into some form of "predestination." Or conversely, when human freedom is overstated in the presence of God, the holy otherness of God becomes easily compromised so that the church settles for an accommodating God of love without acknowledgement of God's uncompromising holiness. Such "unshakeable" claims variously give aid and comfort but represent careless and uncritical conclusions.

But then back to Marx and Engel:

3. The church is also an arena (maybe the last such arena in our town) where unshakeable systems are subject to exposé and contradiction. The study that takes place in a local congregation may evoke critical awareness concerning presumed "givens" that must be kept open to question. In the prayer life of the church, our listening for the voice of the gospel God may bring to us (reveal to us) fresh awarenesses that upset our assured world.

> And of course, the church in its preaching ministry has an opportunity to utter the dismissal of what seems unshakeable all around us.

All of this I had in mind when it came time for the sermon on this Sunday morning. Our senior pastor, Linda, boldly exposited Jeremiah 18:1–11. In this remarkable symmetrical text, Jeremiah has God declare that divine resolve is for plucking up and tearing down and destroying—God's unshakable resolve—is open for review if society repents. Or alternatively if God resolves to build and to plant, but that society does evil, God can reverse course. Thus even divine decree is open to revision, depending on the dialogic interaction between the God who governs and the people who answer to that God. Everything is left open for the decision-making of Israel, so that Israel gets to decide by its actions what may or may not be unshakeable in divine resolve.

Our pastor, on that Sunday, let this tormented reasoning of Jeremiah make contact with the systemic racism in our society. One might indeed judge that systemic racism is an "unshakeable system" among us that evokes divine judgment. But the prophet allows that such divine judgment might not pertain if the community "turns" from its racism. Conversely, if God does good to a society, but it persists in racism, then that positive divine resolve will be altered into devastating judgment.

Our pastor applied the matter of racism in a general way to our societal sin of racist segregation that still pertains, and dared to say that relief from divine judgment requires a societal "turning." That is, in her rendering even systemic racism is an unshakeable system that is open to upending. After that general sketch our pastor linked the matter more specifically to white racism in our area as concerns Native Americans, against whom we have historically practiced abusive segregation, even as we white Christians have done more broadly concerning Black people.

The outcome of this sermonic rendering is the sober news that plucking up and tearing down is in purview for our idolatrous society in its practice of racism. The good news, alternatively, is that there can be, instead, building and planting. That, however, depends on radical turning in attitude, policy and practice. Of course, this is simply church talk. Of course it was heard and witnessed by a quite limited number of persons. But the word had its say. It does not return "empty" (Isa 55:11). It is odd enough that we gather regularly to hear this "upending word" that belongs to the truth practiced by the church.

I thought, as I left church, that our pastor may suggests three enduring tasks for the church:

1. To treasure, reiterate, and interpret the unshakeable claim of the gospel concerning the Crucified-Risen One among us.
2. To critique and expose the unshakeable claims within the church that contradict the gospel.
3. To engage in upending the unshakeable claims and unshakeable systems that do violence to the truth given us in the One Risen and Crucified.

After the sermon, by way of completing the liturgy, we eagerly sang "I Surrender All":

All to Jesus I surrender, all to him I freely give;
I will love and trust him, in his presence daily live.
I surrender all, I surrender all, all to thee, my blessed Savior, I surrender all.
All to Jesus I surrender; humbly at his feet I bow,
worldly pleasures all forsaken; take me Jesus, take me now. (Refrain)
All to Jesus I surrender; make me, Savior wholly thine;
Let me feel the Holy Spirit, truly know that thou art mine. (Refrain)
All to Jesus I surrender; Lord, I give myself to thee;

fill me with thy love and power; let thy blessing fall on me.
(Refrain)
All to Jesus I surrender, now I feel the sacred flame.
O the joy of full salvation! Glory, glory to his name!
I surrender all, I surrender all, I surrender all, all to thee, my blessed Savior, I surrender all.
("I Surrender All," The United Methodist Hymnal, *354)*

Of course, it is not that easy; most likely most of us, as we sang, did not reflect much of what was to be surrendered. But that is the work of the church. We never know when a "connection" is made. That is why our pastors keep at it; and that is why we keep coming back to listen and sing again, over and over. There is so much we whites must surrender. The good news of the prophet is that we have a choice, given the dialogical readiness of the gospel God, to rechoose the "unshakeable" claim of our lives. That faith is the on-going open-ended work of upending and rechoosing. The news is that our faith is not frozen and fixed. It is open to fresh reading when we have courage for truth-telling and truth-living. I was glad, as is most often the case, to have been at church!

Perhaps when we do this all over again, the next time we can respond by singing the rarely sung wondrous hymn derived from Tennyson:

Strong Son of God, Immortal Love,
whom we, that have not seen thy face,
by faith, and faith alone, embrace,
believing where we cannot prove.
Thou wilt not leave us in the dust;
thou madest man, he knows not why,
he thinks he was not made to die:
and thou hast made him: thou are just.
Thou seemest human and divine,

the highest, holiest manhood, thou.
Our wills are ours, we know not how;
our wills are ours, to make them thine.
Our little systems have their day;
they have their day and cease to be;
they are but broken lights of thee,
and thou, O Lord, art more than they.
We have but faith; we cannot know;
for knowledge is of things we see;
and yet we trust it comes from thee,
a beam in darkness; let it grow.
Let knowledge grow from more to more,
but more of reverence in us dwell;
that mind and soul, according well,
May make one music as before.

(Derived from Tennyson, "In Memoriam")

Our little systems: patriarchy, racism, heterosexual domination, nationalism, scholasticism, individualism, to name a few. Our little systems indeed! Our little systems; they have their day and cease to be!

CONCLUSION

THIS COLLECTION OF comments continues my effort to link the claims of biblical faith to the world in which we live. As my title indicates, the general thesis is that *true words* evoke and offer *new life worlds*, that is, new configurations of social reality. There can be no doubt that the Bible witnesses to such generative utterance. The claim goes back as far as the imperative turn of Moses, "Let my people go," to the lyric of Paul concerning the creator God who "calls into existence things that do not exist" (Rom 4:17). Along the way from Moses to Paul we may notice the generative words of Jesus that variously forgive, cure, and transform lives that had shriveled to impotence:

> *Be made clean! (Mark 1:41)*
> *Sir, our sins are forgiven. (Mark 2:5)*
> *Stretch out your hand. (Mark 3:5)*
> *Peace, be still! (Mark 4:39)*
> *Come out of the man, you unclean spirit! (Mark 5:8)*

The earliest church remembered the transformative power of his utterance.

Karl Barth, more than anyone else, has seen how the word is generative of newness. He takes together as articulations of that word the Bible in its revelatory agency, the full embodiment of the word in the life of Jesus, and, most amazingly, the word uttered in preaching. This triad of expressions makes clear that the word of newness has been entrusted to the church.

Of course the church is not the only one that has noticed the generative power of words. Politicians of every ilk have long known that oft-repeated phrasing may conjure a new world, even if the word is false and the world is phony. No one has understood that world-making capacity of the word than has Donald Trump. And long before him, Madison Avenue and the advertising industry have known that reiterated phrases and slogans can create false needs that require the purchase of particular products. Thus we always face the task of sorting out true generative words and those that are false in their manipulative capacity.

In this present collection Conrad Kanagy's skillful editing has helped us to see and make visible the extended list of venues for God's newness: community, governance, worship, economy, earth, and heaven. Indeed, the claim of these comments, in sum, is that God's capacity for newness pertains to every sphere of our life from the mystery of worship to the quotidian reality of the economy. There is no zone of our life that does not wait in need for newness. There is no zone of our life, moreover, where God's utterance does not generate newness.

It is the core claim of gospel faith that in Jesus that word of God became flesh, full of grace and truth. The Gospel narratives attest the specificity and particularity of the ways in which Jesus, in utterance and in action, caused newness. The authorities of Rome and Jewish leadership perceived him as a great and dangerous threat to the old order over which the presided and from which they greatly benefited. The execution of Jesus at the hands of the empire was a final desperate attempt to curb the force of his generative word that upset so many apple carts. Easter, as we know, is the final routing of the power of empire. In Easter the word of life triumphed over every imperial pretense at ultimacy.

It is mind-boggling to entertain the conviction that this uttered, performed word has been entrusted to the church in our feeble faith. And yet, the Christian congregation gathers regularly to hear the word again. We listen to the word of scripture; we listen as the sermon links that scriptural word to our world. And in response, by the gestures of offering and tithe we sign on to enact the word concretely in our life in the world. The church regularly gains energy and resolve to perform that transformative word out of which there comes, always yet again, a new world of wellbeing, truth, mercy, justice, compassion and joy.

The final essay in this collection concerns "unshakeable systems." In the ancient world Rome was an unshakeable imperial system. Pilate, the governor, mobilized all of that unshakeable authority when he commanded the soldiers concerning the tomb of Jesus, "Make it a secure as you can" (Matt 27:65). Like Pilate we all cherish our most reliable systems of security and meaning. In our anxiety we willingly regard them as unshakeable. Sometimes we face unshakable systems on which we rely. Sometimes we face unshakable systems that we bear because they seem beyond change. And then we read again how it was on the Friday of his execution.

> *At that moment the curtain of the temple was torn in two,*
> *from top to bottom. The earth shook, and rocks were split.*
> *The tombs also were opened, and many bodies of the saints*
> *who had fallen asleep were raised. (Matt 27:51–52)*

Even the temple, the most unshakable citadel, was shaken to its foundation. We do not know if we should take the words of Matthew literally or figuratively. Either way, the text asserts that the unshakeable systems of the day were decisively shaken. They could not resist the unspeakable mystery of his death and his Easter to come. Such a moment of upheaval reminds that all of our certitudes are penultimate. Partly such an upheaval is a profound threat. But partly such a shaking of the unshakeable is good news, especially for the forgotten, the left behind, and the disadvantaged. The news is that no such system of advantage and disadvantage is beyond deep revision.

So imagine: the church meets regularly to listen to the word again. We are *recipients* of the word that shatters all of our certitudes. But we are also *performers* of that new word that makes all things new, beginning with our neighborhood. It is enough for us to be "spellbound" (Luke 19:47). It is my hope that these comments will summon us to enter into the zone of "the spellbound" from whence can come new life, new energy, and new courage. It is no wonder that Luther, in his signature hymn, could declare,

> *One little word shall fell him.*
> *That word above all earthly powers,*
> *no thanks to them abideth.*
> *("A Mighty Fortress,"* Glory to God, *275)*

When we receive that word, we may be on our way to

- new community . . . in which they "shall not hurt or destroy" (Isa 65:25);
- new governance . . . where "justice and only justice" shall be pursued (Deut 16:18);
- new worship . . . "in spirit and in truth" (John 4:24);
- new economy . . . "as much as each of them needed" (Exod 16:18);
- a new earth . . . long with "a new earth and a new Jerusalem" (Rev 21:2);
- a new heaven . . . "For I am about to create new heavens and a new earth" (Isa 65:17–18).

We always again are summoned: "Listen up."

Walter Brueggemann